21x 11/13 ษ 6/13

jam it, pickle it, cure it

KAREN SOLOMON

Photography by **JENNIFER MARTINÉ**

jam it, pickle it, cure it

AND OTHER COOKING PROJECTS

TEN SPEED PRESS
Berkeley

Disclaimer: Some of the recipes in this book include raw eggs, meat, or fish. When these foods are consumed raw, there is always the risk that bacteria, which is killed by proper cooking, may be present. For this reason, when serving these foods raw, always buy certified salmonella-free eggs and the freshest meat and fish available from a reliable grocer and store them in the refrigerator until they are served. Because of the health risks associated with the consumption of bacteria that can be present in raw eggs, meat, and fish, these foods should not be consumed by infants, small children, pregnant women, the elderly, or any persons who may be immunocompromised.

Copyright © 2009 by Karen Solomon
Photography copyright © 2009 by Jennifer Martiné

All rights reserved. Published in the United States by Ten Speed Press, an imprint of the Crown Publishing Group, a division of Random House, Inc., New York.
www.crownpublishing.com
www.tenspeed.com

Ten Speed Press and the Ten Speed Press colophon are registered trademarks of Random House, Inc.

Quick Pickled Daikon with Lemon (page 38) appeared originally in the
San Francisco Chronicle.

Library of Congress Cataloging-in-Publication Data on file with publisher.

ISBN 978-1-58008-958-6

Printed in China

Cover and text design by Betsy Stromberg
Food styling by Karen Shinto

11 10 9 8 7 6 5 4 3 2

First Edition

To my mom, Arlene Solomon, the original *balabusta*,
who taught me to take pleasure and refuge in the kitchen.

contents

3 brine it
PICKLES AND OLIVES

4 noodle it
EASY PASTA, THREE WAYS

5 hook it
PRESERVED AND CURED FISH

6 hunt it
PRESERVED AND CURED MEAT

11 unwrap it
MAKING CANDY

12 drink it
HARD AND SOFT BEVERAGES

acknowledgments

My heartfelt gratitude, first and foremost, to my darling Matthew. Almost without exception, you were the sole dish-doer of this entire project. I simply cannot thank you enough for your input, your critiques, and your pot scrubbery. I still owe you deeply for all of those sticky candy pans.

Without Jane Tunks, none of this would have ever happened. Thank you, my dear, for being the butt-kicking inspiration. My gratitude also to Lorena Jones and to Ten Speed, and to my editors, Genoveva Llosa and Clancy Drake.

The incredible team who made these pages so beautiful deserves a round of applause. I am amazed at the chic urban beauty of the photos of Jennifer Martiné, and the incredible, edible craftwork of stylist Karen Shinto. Many thanks to you both.

I also thank my army of testers for their enthusiasm, their input, and their utter patience with a work-in-progress. They are Gregory Schaefer, Eileen O'Neil, Jill Szumacher, Rachella Sinclair, Meghan Elliot, Benjamin Gross, Julie Ross-Godar, and Christine Fronsdal.

Without the wisdom, guidance, and mentoring of Anika Luskin Streitfeld, who has been supportive of me in innumerable ways, I would never have met Danielle Svetcov, her partner in crime, who—quite literally—made my ambition come to fruition. A big bow to you both for your tireless efforts.

And last, I thank my darling Emmett, who spit it out if it wasn't good enough. We should all be lucky enough to have such a humbling critic.

introduction

When I was growing up, the über-processed Miracle Whip—my family's 1978 God-given bath for tuna fish—literally made me gag as it soddened an otherwise respectable sandwich. To my mind, that gooey sweet stuff sitting in jars for untold ages, plagued with the gunk of calcium disodium, low-grade soybean oil, and modified food starch, tainted everything it touched. And today, decades later, post–Chez Panisse, and the organic, Slow Food, and local eating movements, if you peek inside most American pantries, you'll still find them stuffed with prefab food.

Ever since I've presided over my own kitchen larder, I have worked to duck the stranglehold of Big Mayo in my day-to-day culinary life. My delight in experimentation, insatiable food lust, and perseverance helped me think outside the jar. Like any junkie, I have single-mindedly forged my way through homemade salad dressings, baked goods, and, eventually, simple cheeses and sausages. They were good! I got cocky, served it all with pride, and went back to the kitchen for more.

I've now had the pleasure of writing the book that I've looked for in vain for years. I'd always hoped to find those Girl Scout blueprints to the kitchen—the culinary equivalent of knot tying, fire starting, and good citizenship—that would be the building blocks for everyday eating. But usually when I wanted to make for myself the staples we bought at the store—basic mustard, simple crackers, or day-to-day cooking shortening, for example—I'd have to dig through ancient recipe texts, obscure farm manuals, and the food-geek blogosphere. Stocking the pantry and our own refrigerator doors with ingredients that were made by hand for centuries should not be so cumbersome. Here, I hope to share the joy of real, obtainable DIY kitchen crafting projects at their best. I hope you are moved to grab a wooden spoon and a jar because food crafts you can eat and share are fun—way more fun than stringing together a macaroni necklace.

Admittedly, some of these projects are pretty involved, and no one is expecting you to bust out the Kitchen-Aid just for a couple dollops of good salad dressing. But when the desire to get crafty strikes, I want this to be your go-to book. Throughout, I've tried to make the entire creative process as simple, fun, and foolproof as possible, using everyday ingredients and equipment whenever they can serve.

While this book hardly answers the question, "What's for dinner?," it can help you (and your "craftivist" friends) take advantage of your creativity, keeping your pantries and fridges stocked with high quality, sharable staples and reasonably obtained extravagances. I am not a chef, and never would I claim to be. I am, however, curious, creative, inventive, and really into making stuff—stuff I can eat and get others to eat—with my own hands. Mainly I am a crafter and food is my medium of choice. I truly hope that something in these chapters will inspire your own culinary DIY spirit.

Best of luck kicking the lid off Big Mayo.

1 | munch it

CRACKERS, CHIPS, AND DIPS

More often than not, commercially produced store-bought crackers and chips taste about as good as the cardboard box and plastic bag they come in. While in recent years manufacturers have rolled out a wide array of artisanal snacks that are actually worth eating, making your own packs both the satisfaction of accomplishment and the shrewd wink of someone who has saved $8 a box. Plus, you can't beat the delicate flavors and aromas of a fresh snack food crafted from your own hand.

Most of the snacks in this chapter pair well with everything from jam and cheese to dips and spreads. They are a staple for every pantry and easy enough to knock out in a few hours. Stored in an airtight container, crackers and chips keep their crunch for several days—some up to a month—so they can be made in advance and be ready for snacking when you need them most. This is the ultimate kitchen project for the food-minded crafter: easy to assemble, entirely portable, and unexpected (though always appreciated) as a gift or potluck contribution.

basic crackers, breadsticks, and flatbread

Makes about 250 snack crackers, 48 hors d'oeuvre crackers, 24 breadsticks, or 12 flatbreads

TIME COMMITMENT
1 to 4 hours

Do-it-yourself crackers open doors of possibility—not just for ingredients but also for shapes. Slice the cracker dough into 2 by 3-inch rectangles for the perfect hors d'oeuvre vehicles. Cut it into tiny squares and you've got snacks on hand. Shape it into long and skinny strips and, voilà, breadsticks are ready to be dipped into soup or wrapped in prosciutto. Roll it slightly thicker and the size of a sandwich plate, and you've got flatbread ready to hold a host of hearty toppings. If you plan on presenting these as gifts, consider placing them in tied cellophane bags, in paper-covered tin cans, or in decorative boxes.

PREP AHEAD If you want your crackers to look more professional than rustic, have cookie cutters and decorative stamps (never inked and saved for food use only) on hand.

2 cups all-purpose flour, plus more for dusting

1 teaspoon baking powder

1 teaspoon sugar

1 teaspoon kosher salt, plus more for the cracker tops

1/2 teaspoon freshly ground black pepper, plus more for the cracker tops

1 egg

1/3 cup neutral vegetable oil, like canola or sunflower

1/4 to 1/2 cup cold water

INSTRUCTIONS In a large bowl or food processor, mix the 2 cups of flour, baking powder, sugar, 1 teaspoon of salt, and pepper. In another bowl, lightly beat the egg and vegetable oil. Slowly stir the liquid into the dry ingredients in the bowl, or combine in the processor and pulse, until the dough starts to form a coarse meal. Add the water as needed, 1 tablespoon at a time, until the dough comes together and you can form it into a single ball.

On a lightly floured work surface, cut the dough in half. Shape each piece into a square about 12 inches wide. Wrap each piece in plastic wrap and refrigerate for 30 minutes.

Preheat the oven to 375°F. Lightly oil 2 baking sheets and dust with flour.

Roll out 1 piece of dough, trying to retain its square shape, until it reaches a thickness of 1/8 to 1/4 inch. The desired thickness can vary to your taste; note that the thinner the cracker, the crisper and the more delicate it will be. Lightly prick the dough all over, every half inch or so, with the tines of a fork. Lightly brush the top with water, sprinkle with additional salt, pepper, or other flavorings (see Variations below), then give it 1 or 2 more gentle rolls with a floured rolling pin to press the toppings into the dough.

Cut the dough into the desired shape: for tiny snack crackers, score into 1-inch squares; for hors d'oeuvre crackers, cut into 2 by 3-inch rectangles; for breadsticks, cut into long skinny straws; and for flatbread, simply slice the rolled-out dough into 6 equal pieces. For round, or more uniform, stylish crackers, cut them out with a decorative

// CONTINUED

cookie cutter or shot glass. If you're using a decorative stamp, use it now.

Carefully transfer the crackers onto the prepared baking sheets using a scraper or a spatula. Bake for 8 to 20 minutes, until evenly browned. Check the crackers after 8 minutes; their cooking time will vary by size and thickness. Small, snack-size crackers might be ready, whereas flatbread could require longer. Note that all the crackers might not be done at the same time—those around the edges of the baking sheet might cook more quickly.

HOW TO STORE IT Cool the crackers completely, and store in an airtight container up to 1 week or more. These crackers also freeze beautifully for several months. Let them sit at room temperature for 2 hours before use.

VARIATIONS **Rich Cheese Crackers:** Add 3 cups shredded cheese—Cheddar, Asiago, or Parmesan cheese, or any combination thereof—along with 1/4 cup ground almonds and 1 teaspoon powdered mustard after you've mixed the wet ingredients in with the dry.

Rosemary and Olive Oil Crackers: Replace the neutral oil with olive oil, and add 1 teaspoon chopped dried rosemary to the dough after adding the water.

Sesame, Poppy Seed, and Onion Crackers: Sauté about 1 cup minced yellow onion and 1 teaspoon salt in 1 tablespoon vegetable oil over medium-high heat until very brown. Cool slightly and add to the dough before adding the water. Before cutting, top the crackers with 2 tablespoons each poppy seeds and sesame seeds, along with the salt.

baked potato chips

Makes about 5 ounces

TIME COMMITMENT
1 hour

The snack world is rife with doodles, twists, and puffs, but nothing can hold a candle to an honest-to-goodness homemade potato chip. For the full-fat version, skip ahead to the Fried Potato Chips recipe (page 9). If you are among the calorie conscious, this incredibly low-fat option delivers satisfying salt and crunch without the heft of the Fry Daddy. You will need mad knife skills and a surgeon's touch to slice potatoes thin enough by hand, so I recommend a mandoline for the job. Satisfy the snackers in your world with a gift of chips: wrap them in an attractive cellophane bag or a towel-lined basket, and take them to your next social gathering.

1 pound russet or waxy potatoes
Kosher salt

INSTRUCTIONS Preheat the oven to 300°F. Oil 2 large baking sheets with neutral vegetable oil.

Scrub, dry, and slice the potatoes about 1/16 inch thick. Peel them or don't.

Arrange the sliced potatoes in a single layer, covering as much of the sheet as possible, but don't let them touch.

Do the same for the second sheet. Discard any slices that aren't whole or uniform in thickness.

Bake for 40 minutes, or until the chips are thoroughly dried throughout, testing the center of each chip for doneness. Sprinkle with salt to taste.

Transfer to a wire rack and let cool completely.

HOW TO STORE IT Keep chips crisp in a sealable plastic bag or airtight container. They will keep for 1 month.

fried potato chips

Makes about 6 ounces

TIME COMMITMENT
3 hours

Unlike the Baked Potato Chips, these are the real deal: crisp, flavorful, and as good as the ones in a crinkly sack, without the extra packaging and corporate gouging. Stick to russet potatoes, which produce the most crispness and the least amount of splatter. Although I recommend soaking the sliced potatoes in water before cooking them, which will result in superior chips, you can skip this step if your schedule doesn't allow it. An inexpensive candy or frying thermometer, available at cookware stores, is essential to maintain the right temperature, which will keep the taste quotient of these chips flying high. While you can use any large saucepan or deep skillet for frying, I recommend a wok since it provides the greatest surface area for the potatoes while requiring the least amount of oil for frying.

PREP AHEAD Spread plenty of clean kitchen towels or newspapers on a work surface—you will need them to drain and dry the potatoes. In addition, have a large amount of oil on hand: depending on the size of your saucepan or wok, you will likely go through several cups.

1 pound russet potatoes (about 3)
2 to 4 cups vegetable oil
Kosher salt

INSTRUCTIONS Scrub and dry the potatoes. Peel, or don't—I like my chips with the skin on. Slice very thinly, about 1/16 inch thick. You should almost be able to see through them. Let them soak, covered in cold water, for 1 to 2 hours.

Drain and dry thoroughly on clean kitchen towels.

In a wok or deep skillet with a candy or frying thermometer attached, heat at least 2 inches of oil on medium-high heat, adjusting the heat as necessary to keep the oil at 375° to 395°F. While the oil heats up, cover a nearby countertop with plenty of dry newspaper or kitchen towels.

When the oil is ready, make sure the potatoes are completely dry, and add a single layer of potato slices to the hot oil. Fry for 4 to 7 minutes, depending on their thickness, flipping several times with a wooden spoon or spatula, until very brown on both sides. Remove the chips from the oil with a slotted spoon, leaving as much oil behind as possible, and let drain on newspaper or kitchen towels. Sprinkle with salt to taste, or immediately toss with one of the flavor add-on variations (see page 10).

HOW TO STORE IT While still delicious, chips that aren't thoroughly fried will not keep, so make sure each chip is crisp in the middle and completely cooled before storing. Crisp chips will last in an airtight container up to 1 month.

// **CONTINUED**

fried potato chips, CONTINUED

VARIATIONS **Cheese and Herb Chips:** Combine 3 tablespoons nutritional yeast, 3 tablespoons grated Parmesan cheese, 1 1/2 teaspoons dried rosemary, 1 1/2 teaspoons dried oregano, and 1 tablespoon salt in a large sealable plastic bag. While the chips are still warm, but thoroughly drained, place one-third of the chips in the bag at a time and shake well enough to coat. Let them continue to cool and, if desired, add additional salt.

BBQ Potato Chips: In a large sealable plastic bag, combine 1/2 teaspoon cayenne pepper, 1/2 teaspoon liquid smoke, 1 tablespoon molasses, 1 large minced garlic clove (use a garlic press if you have one), and 1 tablespoon kosher salt. While the chips are still warm, but thoroughly drained, place one-third of the chips in the bag at a time and shake well enough to coat. Lay the chips in a single layer to dry and cool thoroughly. If desired, add additional salt.

Sweet Potato Chips: Substitute sweet potatoes for russets. Fry as instructed above (without first soaking in water). Note that they cook faster—in about 3 minutes. Sweet potato chips are more delicate and cannot withstand being shaken with additional ingredients, so simply sprinkle them with salt, sugar, cayenne pepper, or all three.

cheese chips

TIME COMMITMENT
1 hour

These ridiculously addictive snacks are outstanding by themselves or alongside soups, dips, and sauces. The only drawback to making cheese chips is that they smoke like crazy. Your home may be filled with a gray haze, but the results are worth it. Good ventilation and a chef's toque are helpful, but not essential, for keeping cooking odors out of your home and hair. I recommend buying the cheese at your local deli counter and asking them to slice it thick.

6 slices provolone cheese, sliced 1/8 inch thick

INSTRUCTIONS Heat a nonstick frying pan over medium-high heat. Place a single slice of cheese in the center and let sit for about 4 minutes, undisturbed, or until the edges brown and the cheese is bubbly throughout. Flip and let brown on the second side, for 2 to 3 minutes more. Drain on paper towels and cool slightly; the chip will crispen as it cools. Repeat for the remaining chips. Eat as is, or crack into chips. Eat alone or with your favorite dip.

HOW TO STORE IT In your gut. Cheese chips don't stay crispy for more than a couple of hours at room temperature. Make often and eat immediately.

classic black bean dip

Makes 1¹/4 cups

TIME COMMITMENT
30 minutes to 9 hours

Your mom probably served this old-school party dip at a family bar mitzvah or your graduation party. Ignore the fact that it is completely inauthentic to any dip served south of the border. This is pure Americana on a chip. I recommend making the beans from scratch, but in a pinch, canned beans will suffice. And if you find yourself with leftover beans, what a lucky person you are. Add them to soups, stews, and salads.

³/4 cup dried black beans or 1 (15-ounce) can, drained and rinsed

1/3 cup Yogurt Cheese (page 78) or cream cheese

1 clove garlic, minced

3 tablespoons olive oil

2 teaspoons white wine vinegar

1 teaspoon kosher salt

1 teaspoon ground cumin

1/4 teaspoon cayenne pepper

1/4 cup shredded Cheddar cheese (optional)

1/4 cup chopped black olives (optional)

1/4 cup chopped tomato (optional)

INSTRUCTIONS If you are using dried beans, start by cooking them. In a large pot, cover the beans with water and soak them overnight. (Alternatively, boil for 1 minute, turn off the heat, and let sit for 1 hour.) Drain the beans and rinse. Cover with fresh water, put the lid on the pot, and bring to a boil over medium-high heat. Reduce the heat until the water is just simmering and cook for 30 to 45 minutes or more, until the beans are very tender. Drain and cool.

Measure out 1¹/2 cups of cooked beans and place them (or the canned beans, if using) in a bowl. Mash the beans with a fork, then add the yogurt cheese, garlic, olive oil, vinegar, salt, cumin, and cayenne pepper and mix to combine completely. Top with the cheddar cheese, olives, and/or tomato, and serve.

HOW TO STORE IT Don't make more than a day ahead of time, as the garlic will lose its bite. Refrigerate the beans, covered, up to 5 days.

white bean dip

Makes about 1 1/4 cups

TIME COMMITMENT
30 minutes to 9 hours

This classic Italian flavor combination is perfect as a dip for chips or a spread for crusty baguette slices. I recommend making the beans from scratch, as the flavor is just that much more robust and the texture that much more toothsome. If you are short on time, drained, rinsed canned beans will do. Leftover cooked beans may be added to soups, stews, or salads, or may be frozen for later use.

1 cup dried cannellini beans or 1 (15-ounce) can, drained and rinsed

1/4 cup olive oil

4 cloves garlic, thinly sliced

1/4 cup loosely packed chopped fresh sage leaves

Kosher salt and freshly ground black pepper

INSTRUCTIONS If you are using dried beans, start by cooking them. In a large pot, cover the beans with water and soak them overnight. (Alternatively, boil for 1 minute, turn off the heat, and let sit for 1 hour.) Drain the beans and rinse. Cover with fresh water, put the lid on the pot, and bring to a boil over medium-high heat. Reduce the heat until the water is just simmering and cook for 30 to 45 minutes or more, until the beans are very tender. Drain and cool.

Measure out 1 1/2 cups of cooked beans and place them (or the canned beans, if using) in a bowl. Mash the beans with a fork and set aside.

Place a small frying pan over medium heat and add the olive oil. Let it warm, then add the garlic and the sage. Stir constantly for about 4 minutes, or until the garlic is brown (but not burned) and the sage is crispy.

Pour the hot mixture over the beans and stir well. Add salt and pepper to taste.

HOW TO STORE IT Refrigerate, covered, up to 1 week.

2 | bottle it

ALL MANNER OF CONDIMENTS

The simplest foods—be they raw or cooked vegetables, seared chicken breasts, or even the humble cheese sandwich—don black tie and tails when dunked in the right sauce. Without dressing, Caesar salad is just a bunch of lettuce and old bread. And when was the last time you ate any kind of potato au naturel? French fries, home fries, and baked potatoes are a blank canvas for mayonnaise, ketchup, mustard, or hot sauce.

But peek under the lids on the off-the-shelf condiments in your refrigerator and you'll find flabby, flavorless salad topping, gooey sweet sauces, and bland excuses for what great condiments could be. The best thing about them is the useful bottles in which they come. Life is too short for excess soybean oil and xanthan gum—particularly when you can make great condiments from ingredients already on your pantry shelf.

The key to making condiments at home is using the highest-quality ingredients: fresh eggs; ripe, full-flavored herbs and produce; and the very best oil you can buy. Be warned that most homemade condiments are ephemeral beasts and don't stay fresh for more than a week or so. Their flavors mute and often the condiment begins to break down. It's best to make small batches and only what you need for a few days.

infused oil

There are two ways to infuse flavor into oil. You can slowly steep garlic in a neutral oil, such as canola or sunflower, to produce a cleaner-looking infused oil—important if you plan to garnish a food plate with it or present the flavorful oil as a gift. Alternatively, you can blend or process garlic with the oil to quickly produce an infusion that will work perfectly in a salad dressing or homemade mayonnaise (page 27), or as a flavor addition to finished meat, fish, or vegetables. Both methods allow you to exercise your creative muscles in the kitchen.

PREP AHEAD You'll need a clean jar or bottle to store the infused oil. Make sure it is free of rust and odors and the lid seals tightly. Prepare a label that lists the contents and date prepared.

   4 cloves garlic, peeled
   1 cup best-quality neutral vegetable oil, like canola or sunflower

INSTRUCTIONS **The fast method:** In a blender or food processor, mince the garlic, then add the oil and blend or process for 30 seconds. Let sit for 30 minutes. Strain, and press down on the solids before discarding them.

   The slow method: Mince the garlic cloves and combine with the oil in a jar. Cover tightly, and store in a cool dark place for 2 weeks, gently swirling the contents every 2 days. Strain, and press down on the solids before discarding them.

HOW TO STORE IT Refrigerate flavored oils, covered. Oils infused using the fast method will keep for 1 week, while those infused using the slow method will keep up to 2 months.

VARIATIONS For the garlic, substitute 1 cup firmly packed fresh basil leaves (or any other fresh herb); or the zest of 1 orange (or 2 lemons or limes); or 4 inches of fresh ginger, chopped; or 2 serrano chiles (see page 18).

basic vinaigrette

Makes about 1/2 cup

TIME COMMITMENT
10 minutes

This vinaigrette is the stuff that French dinner party fantasies are made of. Traditionally, vinaigrette is made at the bottom of the salad bowl and tossed with all the clean and dry salad vegetables just before serving, usually after the main course. Vinaigrette is easy enough to make as needed; I don't recommend storing it for too long because it loses its character and bite after a couple of days. Even the most banal greens will bask in the afterglow of this piquant palate cleanser. A crusty baguette is the best way to soak up each and every drop.

PREP AHEAD You'll need a small clean bottle if you're storing the dressing. Make sure it is free of rust and odors and the lid seals tightly. Prepare a label that lists the contents and date prepared.

- 1 large clove garlic, minced
- 2 teaspoons kosher salt
- 2 teaspoons powdered mustard
- 1/2 cup plus 1 tablespoon extra virgin olive oil
- 2 tablespoons freshly squeezed lemon juice, balsamic vinegar, or white wine vinegar
- Freshly ground black pepper

INSTRUCTIONS Mince the garlic by hand or crush with a garlic press and transfer it to a mortar or the bottom of a wooden bowl. Add the salt, and with the pestle or the back of a sturdy spoon grind the salt into the garlic until it forms a paste. Don't rush this step of the process, as this is the flavor base for your dressing. Make sure that all of the salt is incorporated and mashed into the garlic until pasty.

Stir in the mustard and the 1 tablespoon of olive oil. Combine well. Again, don't rush, since this is how your dressing will get its smooth consistency.

Once the oil is fully incorporated into the garlic and salt paste, add the remaining 1/2 cup olive oil, a little at a time, stirring to combine as you go. Then add the lemon juice and pepper to taste. Stir well and taste again, adjusting the seasoning as necessary.

HOW TO STORE IT Refrigerate, tightly covered, up to 3 days.

severely hot (or not) sauce

Makes about 3½ cups

TIME COMMITMENT
Less than 1 hour

Some foods, like Vietnamese spring rolls, Mexican tacos, and Indian curries, just ache for blazing heat, and this saucy little condiment will indeed ignite the flame. Since this recipe produces a hot sauce that hits zowie on the heat scale, it is not for heat novices. If you want yours a little tamer, use all jalapeños, substitute a milder poblano or pasilla chile for the serranos, or use just half jalapeño and half bell peppers. When handling hot chiles, proceed with caution: wear plastic gloves and protective goggles and work in a well-ventilated area. When cut with a knife or pureed in a blender, the chiles can emit irritants that cause coughing or mild choking and are difficult to wash off your hands. Make certain to wash your knife and cutting board thoroughly afterward to avoid adding heat to your next recipe.

PREP AHEAD You'll need clean jars or bottles to store the hot sauce. Make sure they are free of rust and odors and the lids seal tightly. Prepare a label that lists the contents and date prepared.

- 1 pound jalapeño chiles
- 1 pound serrano chiles
- 3 cloves garlic, peeled
- 2 tablespoons plus 1 teaspoon kosher salt
- 2¼ cups distilled white vinegar
- 4 tablespoons sugar

INSTRUCTIONS Wash and dry the chiles, and remove the stems. Slice them in half lengthwise (please see caution note above about working with chiles). Either grill or broil, outside skin near the flame, until black and charred. The timing on this will vary depending on your heat and the size of the chiles. You may need to work in multiple batches to cook them all.

In a food processor or blender, puree the garlic until minced. Add the chiles, salt, vinegar, and sugar, and puree for about 3 minutes, or until very well combined.

Transfer to a glass jar and refrigerate.

HOW TO STORE IT Refrigerate, covered, up to several months. It will slowly lose its heat over time.

regular ol' tomato ketchup (but better)

Makes about 3 cups

TIME COMMITMENT
Less than 1 hour

If you're craving the taste of that red stuff that comes with a burger at your favorite fast food restaurant, this recipe is bound to disappoint. This ketchup has a stronger flavor and a tangier sweet and vinegary taste than its cousin laden with xanthan gum and corn syrup. However, it's still the best thing to happen to French fries since the potato.

PREP AHEAD You'll need a clean jar to store the ketchup. Make sure it is free of rust and odors and the lid seals tightly. Prepare a label that lists the contents and date prepared.

- 1 cinnamon stick
- 1 bay leaf
- 5 whole cloves
- 5 cardamom pods, crushed
- 1 star anise
- 10 black peppercorns
- 1 (28-ounce) can whole tomatoes
- 1 large yellow onion, quartered
- 2 tablespoons neutral vegetable oil, like canola or sunflower
- 2 teaspoons kosher salt, plus more to taste
- 1/3 cup firmly packed golden brown sugar
- 1/2 cup champagne vinegar
- 1 teaspoon Hungarian paprika
- Freshly ground black pepper

INSTRUCTIONS Using a piece of cheesecloth (or an empty tea bag), tie the cinnamon, bay, cloves, cardamom, anise, and peppercorns into a bundle. Set aside.

Pour the tomatoes and their juice into a food processor or blender. Puree until totally smooth, and set aside all but about 1/4 cup. To the remainder, add the onion and puree.

In a large nonreactive Dutch oven (bigger than you think, as this will splatter like a Pollock painting), heat the oil over medium-high heat. Add the onion puree and the 2 teaspoons of salt and stir well. Cook for 8 to 10 minutes, letting the puree reduce and lightly brown. Add the tomato, sugar, and vinegar, turn the heat to a low simmer, and reduce for about 15 minutes, uncovered, with an occasional stir. Add the spice bundle and reduce for 10 minutes more. When it's done reducing, it should be a little thinner than commercial ketchup. Stir in the paprika, taste for seasoning, and adjust as needed.

Let the ketchup cool and remove the spice bundle. Pour into a jar and chill overnight, or for at least 6 hours.

HOW TO STORE IT Refrigerated, homemade ketchup will keep at least 2 months.

HOW TO CAN IT Carefully read through the canning directions on page 88 before you begin. Ladle into sterilized half-pint jars, leaving 1/4 inch headspace, and process in a hot-water bath for 15 minutes at altitudes up to 1,000 feet, 20 minutes at altitudes up to 6,000 feet, and 25 minutes at altitudes over 6,000 feet.

orange yogurt dressing

Makes about 1 1/4 cups

TIME COMMITMENT
10 minutes

Slightly fruitier and lighter in calories than a traditional vinaigrette, this creamy dressing offers a nice tang and is especially great with peppery greens like arugula. The beauty of this and other creamy dressings is that they stay fresh longer and may be used throughout the week. This dressing tastes particularly good when made with homemade orange marmalade (page 92), but of course a store-bought version will suffice.

PREP AHEAD You'll need a small clean bottle to store the dressing. Make sure it is free of rust and odors and the lid seals tightly. Prepare a label that lists the contents and date prepared.

1 clove garlic, minced

1 teaspoon kosher salt, plus more to taste

3 tablespoons extra virgin olive oil

3/4 cup plain yogurt

4 1/2 teaspoons freshly squeezed lemon juice or white wine vinegar

3 tablespoons Orange Marmalade (page 92)

Freshly ground black pepper

INSTRUCTIONS In the bottom of a large salad bowl or mortar, mash the garlic into the 1 teaspoon of salt until it forms a paste. Add the olive oil, and stir thoroughly until it emulsifies. Add the yogurt, lemon juice, and marmalade, and stir thoroughly to combine. Season with pepper, taste, and adjust as needed.

HOW TO STORE IT Refrigerate, covered, up to 5 days.

oregano and cumin dressing

Makes about 1 cup

TIME COMMITMENT
10 minutes

Here is a great salad dressing for shredded cabbage, jicama, apples, onions, or any kind of slaw. Oregano and cumin, dominant spices in Cuban cuisine, also pair well with citrusy and spicy foods. For a slightly less acidic and sweeter version of this dressing, use orange juice instead of lime juice.

PREP AHEAD You'll need a small clean bottle to store the dressing. Make sure it is free of rust and odors and the lid seals tightly. Prepare a label that lists the contents and date prepared.

  1 clove garlic, minced
  1 teaspoon kosher salt
  1/2 cup neutral vegetable oil, like canola or sunflower
  1 tablespoon fresh oregano, chopped
  1 1/2 teaspoons ground cumin
  3/4 cup freshly squeezed lime juice (from about 3 to 6 limes)

INSTRUCTIONS In the bottom of a large salad bowl or in a mortar, mash the garlic with the salt until it forms a paste. Add the oil slowly, and combine well until it becomes cohesive and cloudy. Add the oregano, cumin, and lime juice, and combine completely.

HOW TO STORE IT Refrigerate, covered, up to 5 days.

tahini goddess dressing

Makes about 1 cup

TIME COMMITMENT
10 minutes

I used to have an addiction to a store-bought version of this classic salad dressing—until I cracked the code and learned to make it. It's remarkably easy, and it keeps its fresh taste longer than many homemade dressings. Skip the water to convert this dressing into a great dip for crudités. The principal ingredient, tahini, is also known as sesame butter.

PREP AHEAD You'll need a small clean bottle to store the dressing. Make sure it is free of rust and odors and the lid seals tightly. Prepare a label that lists the contents and date prepared.

- 2 cloves garlic, minced
- 1 teaspoon kosher salt
- 1/2 cup tahini
- 4 teaspoons soy sauce
- 2 tablespoons apple cider vinegar
- 2 teaspoons honey
- 1/3 cup water
- 2 tablespoons chopped fresh parsley

INSTRUCTIONS In a small bowl with the back of a spoon (or with a mortar and pestle), mash the garlic and salt together until they form a paste. Add the tahini, soy sauce, vinegar, and honey and combine. Add the water 1 teaspoon at a time—just enough to make it pourable. Stir in the parsley.

HOW TO STORE IT Use immediately, or refrigerate, covered, up to 1 week.

buttermilk dressing

Makes about 1 cup

TIME COMMITMENT
10 minutes

Where does buttermilk dressing end and ranch dressing begin? It's a fine line indeed. Both are light, cream-based dressings that are heavily herbed and extremely versatile—and they are virtually interchangeable. If you don't have buttermilk, make your own by mixing 1 teaspoon white vinegar with 1/2 cup whole milk. Or, if you make your own butter (page 76), you will have fresh buttermilk on hand.

PREP AHEAD You'll need a small clean bottle to store the dressing. Make sure it is free of rust and odors and the lid seals tightly. Prepare a label that lists the contents and date prepared.

- 1 large clove garlic, minced
- 1 teaspoon kosher salt
- 2 tablespoons Mayonnaise (page 27)
- 2 tablespoons plain yogurt
- 1 teaspoon powdered mustard
- 1/2 cup buttermilk
- 2 tablespoons chopped green onion
- 1 1/2 teaspoons fresh thyme leaves, or 1/2 teaspoon dried thyme

INSTRUCTIONS In a small bowl with the back of a spoon (or with a mortar and pestle), mash the garlic and salt together until they form a paste. Combine with the mayonnaise, yogurt, and mustard. Slowly add the buttermilk, and stir well to blend. Toss in the onion and thyme. Stir, and refrigerate for 30 minutes or more to allow the flavors to meld.

HOW TO STORE IT Refrigerate, covered, up to 1 week.

caesar dressing

Makes about 1/2 cup

TIME COMMITMENT
15 minutes

All hail Caesar! On any given day, in any run-of-the-mill office, 42 percent of the employees are eating a chicken Caesar salad for lunch. While not exactly scientifically proved, the fact is that this is one of our nation's most popular salad dressings. It pays to make your own so it's rife with flavor and good ingredients.

PREP AHEAD You'll need a small clean bottle to store the dressing. Make sure it is free of rust and odors and the lid seals tightly. Prepare a label that lists the contents and date prepared.

1 large egg

1 small clove garlic

1/2 teaspoon kosher salt

3 anchovy fillets

2 tablespoons Mayonnaise (page 27)

5 teaspoons freshly squeezed lemon juice

1/4 cup extra virgin olive oil

3 tablespoons freshly grated Parmesan cheese

INSTRUCTIONS First, coddle the egg by bringing it to a boil in a small saucepan with just enough water to cover. Once it reaches a rapid boil, cook for 1 minute. Remove the egg from the heat, and immediately run it under cold water until it's cool enough to handle.

Crack the egg into a food processor or blender, and scrape out the white bits from the inside of the shell. Add the garlic, salt, anchovy, mayonnaise, and lemon juice and puree for 1 minute. Drizzle in the olive oil slowly while blending for 1 minute more. Add the cheese and blend just until combined.

HOW TO STORE IT Refrigerate, covered, up to 3 days.

mustard

Makes about 1 cup

TIME COMMITMENT
2 to 3 weeks

Mustard is incredibly easy to prepare; its only drawback is the time commitment, as there's no rushing the 2 to 3 weeks necessary for the flavors to meld and for the mustard to mellow. Taste it when it's freshly assembled and you will be aghast at its bitterness. I promise that your patience will pay off into something hot dog–worthy within the calendar month. Powdered mustard is often overpriced at supermarkets. You can save a few dollars by buying it at Indian or specialty markets, where it can sometimes be found in bulk bins. Don't buy seeds to grind your own powder—the results are inferior to the bought spice.

PREP AHEAD You'll need a small clean jar to store the mustard. Make sure it is free of rust and odors and the lid seals tightly. Prepare a label that lists the contents and date prepared.

> 1/2 cup powdered mustard
> 1/4 cup sugar
> 1/4 cup distilled white vinegar
> 1 teaspoon kosher salt

INSTRUCTIONS Combine all the ingredients in a small bowl. Cover and store in a cool, dark place. Taste after 2 weeks. If it's still too bitter, leave it alone for another week. Once ready to eat, scrape into a bottle and refrigerate.

HOW TO STORE IT Refrigerate, covered, up to 3 months. If your mustard separates, simply stir it back together again.

VARIATIONS **Hot Mustard:** To add heat or gusto to this or any of the mustards below, add any or all of the following: 1 tablespoon minced ginger; 1 clove garlic, minced; 1/2 teaspoon wasabi powder; 1/2 teaspoon cayenne pepper.

Brown Sugar Mustard: Substitute dark brown sugar for the granulated sugar, and red wine vinegar for the white wine vinegar to create a heartier, darker mustard with a rich flavor from the molasses in the sugar.

Honey and Lime Mustard: Substitute 1/2 cup honey for the sugar and fresh lime juice for the white wine vinegar. This mustard is on the sweeter side and makes a great base for a meat marinade or the perfect spread for a ham or pork loin sandwich.

Wine and Fruit Mustard: Substitute 1/4 cup sweet fruit jam, such as Strawberry Jam (page 86), for the sugar and red wine for the white wine vinegar. The wine gives this mustard a stronger bite and a lovely russet color.

Mustard Sauce: In a bowl, combine 6 tablespoons prepared mustard with 6 tablespoons olive oil, 1 tablespoon sugar, 1 tablespoon white wine vinegar, 3 tablespoons chopped fresh dill, and 3 tablespoons Mayonnaise (page 27). This sauce lends better to dipping and drizzling than spreading, and it's a knockout mixed in with tuna or salmon salad, poured over sardines, or served with Gravlax (page 54).

mayonnaise

Makes about 1 cup

TIME COMMITMENT
15 minutes

Julia Child taught us that real mayonnaise makes a real difference. Once you've had a taste of it, you won't be able to go back to the commercially produced stuff. While I love mayo that has been made by vigorous whisking (see variation), a food processor or blender will be happy to do the work for you and save you from repetitive strain injury. This sauce is a kitchen workhorse; it's a great vegetable dip, a meat or fish accompaniment, the bind for egg salad or tuna salad, and—when thinned with water, juice, or added vinegar—a fine salad dressing.

PREP AHEAD You'll need a clean jar to store the mayonnaise. Make sure it is free of rust and odors and the lid seals tightly. Prepare a label that lists the contents and date prepared.

  1 large egg, at room temperature

  1/2 teaspoon prepared Mustard (page 26)

  1 teaspoon kosher salt

  2 teaspoons freshly squeezed lemon juice (from about 1/2 lemon)

  1 cup neutral oil, like canola or sunflower

INSTRUCTIONS Combine the egg, mustard, and salt in a food processor or blender for 30 seconds. Add the lemon juice, and process for 30 seconds more. With the motor running, slowly spoon in 1/2 teaspoon of the oil, and process for 30 seconds. Spoon in another 1/2 teaspoon of the oil, and process for another 30 seconds. The mixture should be emulsified, meaning it looks cloudy throughout and it coats the inside of the bowl evenly. A spoonful at a time, slowly add about half of the remaining oil, and process for another 30 seconds. Drizzle in the remaining oil until the mayonnaise becomes thick and creamy.

HOW TO STORE IT Refrigerate, covered, up to 4 days.

VARIATIONS **Traditional Mayonnaise:** Classic mayonnaise is made with egg yolks (no white). In a bowl, whisk together 1 yolk with the mustard, salt, and lemon juice. Add the oil very slowly, using a teaspoon, continuously whisking until it's smooth and creamy.

Garlic Mayonnaise: Substitute apple cider vinegar for the lemon juice and 1 cup garlic-infused oil (page 16) plus 2 tablespoons canola oil for the oil. After blending the egg, mustard, salt, and vinegar, drizzle 1/2 teaspoon of canola oil very slowly to emulsify the mixture, and process for 30 seconds. Spoon another 1/2 teaspoon of canola oil, process for 30 seconds, and slowly add the remaining canola oil. Add the infused oil very slowly, a tablespoon at a time, taking breaks often to allow it to be incorporated. Add 1 tablespoon chopped black olive and 2 teaspoons chopped small capers to the garlic mayonnaise for an extraordinary accompaniment to canned tuna.

Spicy Sesame Ginger Mayonnaise: Use 1/2 cup canola oil, 4 tablespoons ginger oil (page 16), 3 tablespoons serrano chile oil (page 16), and 1 tablespoon

// CONTINUED

mayonnaise, CONTINUED

toasted sesame oil. Add the flavored oils after you've drizzled all the canola oil into the mayonnaise.

Horseradish and Green Onion Mayonnaise: Combine the basic mayonnaise with 1 teaspoon grated horseradish and 1 tablespoon minced green onion and refrigerate for 30 minutes. This spread is delicious with roast beef or on a roast beef sandwich.

Green Olive and Rosemary Mayonnaise: Combine the basic mayonnaise with 1 tablespoon chopped green olives and 1 teaspoon chopped fresh rosemary and refrigerate for 30 minutes. Try this with flaky white fish like red snapper, halibut, or tilapia.

Tartar Sauce: Combine the basic mayonnaise with 2 tablespoons chopped dill pickles, 1 tablespoon chopped capers, 1 teaspoon minced fresh thyme, and 1 teaspoon minced lemon zest and refrigerate for 30 minutes. This classic dipping sauce is perfect with fried fish.

3 | brine it

PICKLES AND OLIVES

Salt is a wondrous thing; many chefs think of it as their most prized ingredient. Its ability to transform food is a miracle of culinary science that we will explore in the easy-to-make olive and pickle recipes in this chapter.

You do not need a batch of fancy equipment, a barrel of sticky wax, or supreme culinary skills to pickle and brine. It needn't take all day and a farmhouse kitchen of labor. In fact, it's one of the simplest ways to prolong your seasonal produce. While more often than not pickles are ready in just a few days, they can sometimes be ready in only a couple of hours, or can take as long as a few weeks. And the patient student of salt will be rewarded with some of the best olives you've ever tasted and crisp, acidic cold vegetables that add bite and tang to any meal. Nowhere will you find the addition of artificial colors or the heft of too much sugar that is typical in mass-produced canned products. The best part is that a little work now will pay off with brined, chilled, and pickled results later.

Brining is one of humanity's oldest kitchen projects, and one that's more than ready to shake off its old shawls. Pucker up, sweetie, and get that salt-shaker a-shakin'.

pickled green beans

Makes 3 pints

TIME COMMITMENT
3 days

A Bloody Mary without this must-have garnish would be a lonely brunch cocktail, aching for the snap, salt, and brine of these crisp and piquant pickles. The ingredients for this recipe aren't complicated—you probably have the spices on hand—and in a few short minutes of assembly you'll have fresh, flavor-forward pickles on hand for weeks to come. If green beans aren't your thing, you can use this recipe to pickle cucumber spears, carrot sticks, small cauliflower florets, or—for the bold and zesty among you—whole garlic cloves.

PREP AHEAD You'll need 3 clean pint jars with lids. You can buy canning jars with vacuum-seal lids (look for Ball or Kerr brand jars), or you can reuse jars from your pantry. If your jars aren't new, make sure they are free of rust and odors and the lids seal tightly. When it comes to labeling, I'm a strip-of-masking-tape-and-black-Sharpie kind of a gal. However, if you are artistically inclined, feel free to create nifty labels either on stickers or tied around the mouth of the jar. Fancy or not, it's important that you prepare some kind of label that lists the contents and date prepared.

3 pounds green beans, stems intact, washed and dried

9 cloves garlic, crushed

3 cinnamon sticks

3 bay leaves

3 tablespoons yellow mustard seeds

3 tablespoons brown mustard seeds

6 tablespoons dill seeds

3 tablespoons black peppercorns

6 teaspoons kosher salt

$1^1/2$ to $2^1/4$ cups distilled white vinegar

INSTRUCTIONS Add one-third of the green beans, garlic, spices, and salt to each jar. Fill each jar halfway with vin-egar (about $1/2$ to $3/4$ cups). Top off each jar with cool water. Seal each jar with a lid, and shake gently to dissolve the salt and distribute the spices. Refrigerate for at least 3 days.

HOW TO STORE IT Refrigerated pickled green beans will be at their prime for 2 weeks but will keep for about 1 month.

HOW TO CAN IT Carefully read through the canning directions on page 88 before you begin. In a nonreactive saucepan, combine the vinegar, 6 cups water, and the salt and bring to a rolling boil to dissolve the salt. Divide the beans, garlic, bay leaves, and spices evenly among 3 sterilized pint jars as directed, leaving about 1-inch headspace. Pour the boiling vinegar solution into the jars, immersing the beans fully and leaving $1/2$ inch headspace. Process in a hot-water bath for 10 minutes at altitudes up to 1,000 feet, 15 minutes at altitudes up to 6,000 feet, and 20 minutes at altitudes over 6,000 feet.

VARIATION For super-duper garlic pickles, substitute 6 cloves crushed garlic and 4 extra tablespoons of dill seeds for the cinnamon, bay leaves, and mustard seeds. Vampires need not apply.

olives

Makes 3 pounds

TIME COMMITMENT
About 6 weeks

Curing olives is extremely easy: they practically cure themselves. Salt, water, and time are all that's required to craft one of our most popular cocktail snacks to date. Olives fresh off the tree are available in the late fall, often around November. But finding these ripe, but uncured orbs, even seasonally, can be a challenge. If your local farmers' market or specialty or health foods stores don't carry them, contact local small-scale olive producers and ask if they'll sell or mail-order some of their uncured stash. The Olive Oil Source web site (www.oliveoilsource.com) has a list of all U.S. growers of olives for olive oil. Depending on the harvest, some may be willing to ship a small order. Of course, if you are fortunate enough to live in a warm, dry climate, ask everyone you know for friends with olive trees.

PREP AHEAD You'll need a large bowl, bucket, or gallon pitcher to cure the olives, and clean jars to store them in once they're finished. Make sure they are free of rust and odors and the lids seal tightly. Cured olives make wonderful gifts, so choose pretty jars and prepare decorative labels that list the contents and date prepared.

1 cup kosher salt

1 gallon cool water

3 pounds green or black uncured olives

INSTRUCTIONS To make the brine, put the salt in a large bowl, add the water, and stir until dissolved. Wash the olives and, with a sharp knife, make a single cut, down to the pit, along the long side of every olive. Submerge the olives in the brine and weight them down. If you're using a large bowl, an inverted dinner plate will usually suffice. Cover and store in a cool, dark place.

Stir the olives once a week, and remove any scum that has formed on the top. After 6 weeks, start tasting. The olives should no longer be bitter. Note, however, that they can survive in the brine and continue to mellow their flavor for several months.

HOW TO STORE IT The cured olives should be stored in the refrigerator in clean brine solution made from combining 1/2 cup salt with 1 gallon water (half as salty as the curing brine). Or, if you find the olives too salty after brining, store them in jars of plain tap water in the refrigerator. They will last this way for at least 6 months.

VARIATIONS To dress up cured olives for fancy service, remove from the liquid and toss with finishing salt, extra virgin olive oil, lemon juice, orange juice, minced garlic, or dried chile flakes.

stuffed olives

Makes 2 cups

TIME COMMITMENT
1 to 2 hours

If you can't make your own olives, you can still win DIY points by stuffing store-bought olives yourself. Buy large, firm, high-quality brined green or black olives from a gourmet market. If you can find these without pits, consider yourself fortunate. More often than not, good olives come with the pit, which means you and your olive pitter will have to spend some quality time together. Nothing can replace an olive pitter, which can also remove the stones from cherries. They are inexpensive and widely available in kitchenware stores.

PREP AHEAD You'll need clean jars to store the stuffed olives. Make sure they are free of rust and odors and the lids seal tightly. Even if they are not home-cured, stuffed olives are still giftworthy. For an instant gift, choose pretty jars or prepare decorative labels that list the contents and date prepared.

1 large red bell pepper
2 cups cured olives, drained, brine reserved

INSTRUCTIONS Wash and dry the pepper completely. If you have a gas stove, firmly skewer the stem of the pepper with a dinner fork and roast the pepper over the open flame of your gas burner until the skin is completely black and charred, being careful not to set the pepper (or the house) on fire. The barbecue grill is also a delicious way to blacken the skin. If neither of these options is available to you, slice the pepper lengthwise and remove the stems and seeds, and broil the pepper, skin side up, until it is completely charred.

Once cooked and cool enough to handle, use a paper towel to gently rub off the skin and as much of the blackness as possible. Reserve any remaining juice and add this to your reserved olive brine. Slice the pepper into long, thin strips, then chop to the length appropriate for your olives. Insert a piece of pepper into each olive.

HOW TO STORE IT Serve immediately, or refrigerate, covered in brine, up to 1 month. If the olives were store-bought, use the brine they came packed in. If the olives are homemade, use a weak brine solution of 2 tablespoons kosher salt dissolved in 4 cups water.

VARIATIONS **Blue Cheese–Stuffed Olives:** Substitute 1/2 teaspoon (or as much as needed to stuff the olive) crumbled blue cheese for the bell pepper.

Garlic-Stuffed Olives: Substitute fresh garlic slices for the bell pepper.

Anchovy-Stuffed Olives: Substitute chopped anchovies for the bell pepper.

Almond-Stuffed Olives: Substitute whole roasted and salted almonds for the bell pepper.

Parmesan-Stuffed Olives: Substitute Parmesan cheese, cut into 1/16-inch cubes, for the bell pepper.

Butter-Stuffed Olives (yes, butter): Substitute very cold salted or unsalted butter (page 76), cut into 1/16-inch cubes, for the bell pepper.

// CONTINUED

stuffed olives, CONTINUED

Tomato-Stuffed Olives: Substitute cherry tomatoes, cut into spears, for the bell pepper.

Caper-Stuffed Olives: Substitute 1 or 2 capers for the bell pepper.

Raisin-Stuffed Olives: Substitute 1 or 2 raisins for the bell pepper.

Dried Apricot–Stuffed Olives: Substitute dried apricot, cut into thin slivers, for the bell pepper.

Combination-Stuffed Olives: Replace the bell pepper with a combination of any of the above substitutions, such as tomato and butter, raisins and capers, garlic and anchovies, almond and Parmesan, and blue cheese and bell pepper.

super-fast thai cucumber salad

Makes 2 cups

TIME COMMITMENT
Less than 1 hour

This is a tangy-sweet pickle that takes minutes to put together and works as a great complement to spicy curries, noodles, and fried rice. Its color makes it quite an attractive addition to an elegant plate. Plan to eat this one quickly, since it's at its best when eaten within a day or two.

1 English cucumber, or 2 regular cucumbers, peeled, seeded, and thinly sliced (about 2 cups)

1 small red onion, thinly sliced (about 3/4 cup)

2 teaspoons sugar

2 teaspoons kosher salt

1/2 cup unseasoned rice vinegar

INSTRUCTIONS Toss all the ingredients together in a bowl, and let stand for 30 minutes.

HOW TO STORE IT This is meant to be eaten immediately, but leftovers can be refrigerated, covered, up to 2 days.

quick pickled daikon with lemon

Makes 2 cups

TIME COMMITMENT
About 2 hours

Daikon is a mammoth, mild, crunchy Japanese radishy thing that grows like a weed in the winter months and is available in many Asian markets. Its jicama-like crunch lends itself really nicely to a brine. This pickled daikon is more zingy than spicy, making it a fine foil for fish or chicken or spicy tofu. To slice very thinly, use a mandoline if you have one.

PREP AHEAD You'll need a clean pint jar with a lid. Make sure it is free of rust and odors and the lid seals tightly. Prepare a label that lists the contents and date prepared.

1 1/2 pounds daikon, peeled and very thinly sliced

1/4 cup kosher salt

1 teaspoon toasted sesame oil

1 tablespoon honey

1 tablespoon seasoned rice vinegar

1/3 cup freshly squeezed lemon juice

1 clove garlic, minced

3 (2-inch) pieces lemon zest

INSTRUCTIONS Put the daikon in a large colander set over a bowl or in the sink. Toss it with the salt; your hands are the best tools for this job. Let rest for 15 minutes to express some of the excess moisture.

Meanwhile, whisk the sesame oil, honey, vinegar, lemon juice, and garlic in a large bowl.

Rinse the daikon well under running water, then spread it out to dry on a clean kitchen towel, rolling it up gently so as to extract as much moisture as possible. Add the daikon to the brine along with the zest and coat well, letting it marinate for 1 hour.

HOW TO STORE IT Eat immediately, or refrigerate, covered, up to 1 month.

kimchee

Makes 5 pints

TIME COMMITMENT
1 to 3 days

This pungent Korean condiment makes every dish taste better—from stir-fries to eggs, rice, sushi, frittatas, and roast beef sandwiches. Unlike other pickling recipes in this chapter, kimchee is a fermented pickle that not only takes its flavors from its core ingredients but also from natural bacteria in the air. Its flavor and aroma are quite strong and, like aged cheese or Fritos, you either love it or you don't. You can find huge, inexpensive sacks of Korean dried chile flakes at Asian markets or order them online at www.koamart.com. Alternatively, Korean dried chile flakes can be replaced with about one-third as much cayenne pepper, but the flavor won't be quite the same. Obviously, if you can't take the heat of spicy food, don't add as much fuel to this fire.

PREP AHEAD You'll need clean jars with lids. Make sure they are free of rust and odors and the lids seal tightly. Prepare a label that lists the contents and date prepared.

- 3 large heads Napa cabbage, chopped into 2-inch pieces
- 1 cup kosher salt
- 10 cloves garlic, sliced
- 1 (2-inch) piece ginger, peeled and minced
- 1 cup Korean dried chile flakes
- 1 bunch green onions, sliced

INSTRUCTIONS Put the cabbage in a large colander set over a bowl or in the sink. Toss the cabbage with the salt; your hands are the best tools for this job. Let sit for about 40 minutes to express some of the excess moisture.

You'll notice that your cabbage has decreased in volume. Dump the liquid in the bowl, rinse off the excess salt, and pat the cabbage dry with a clean kitchen towel.

// CONTINUED

kimchee, CONTINUED

Pour the cabbage into a clean bowl and add the garlic, ginger, chile flakes, and green onions. Toss well. Loosely cover, and let it sit overnight or longer, up to 3 days, with the flavor growing more intense and fermented. Stir and taste every 12 hours or so, and move on to the next step when the flavor is to your liking. Note that it will release a most fragrant perfume and a good amount of liquid. Both are desired effects.

Pack the kimchee tightly into the jars, including enough liquid to cover all the solids. If you need more liquid, add the smallest amount of cool tap water possible.

HOW TO STORE IT Refrigerate, covered, immersed in the brine, up to 2 months.

VARIATION Substitute 2-inch chunks peeled daikon for the cabbage.

EASY PASTA, THREE WAYS

People go crazy over Italian pastas, waxing poetic about the difference between *gemelli* and *fusilli*, or breaking out geometric tools to pinpoint the minutiae of *rotini* versus *spiralini*. I'm a low-frills, bring-on-the-yum kind of gal, and my favorite pasta shape is the rustic dog that I've made myself. While many home cooks spend hours making their own *ragù*, most feel daunted by the task of making their own noodles and are too easily put off by the fear of not crafting the perfect pasta shape.

To you, I say hogwash. Let your culinary inhibitions fly free. The truth is that few special skills or fancy tools are required to make your own noodles. It takes only some flour, some eggs, and a rolling pin to have your pasta pot running over. The only things that are truly required to make pasta are patience, time, and the willingness to work those upper body muscles. Better still is that homemade pasta keeps like a champ: it can be frozen fresh or dried. This chapter also contains a workaday tomato sauce and a versatile meat, cheese, and vegetable filling—the building blocks of many an Italian meal.

basic pasta dough

Makes 4 (12-inch square)
sheets of dough

TIME COMMITMENT
About 1 hour

I absolutely love homemade egg pasta. It's more rich and flavorful than the mass-produced stuff you buy in a cardboard box. Even though the dough in this recipe is not traditional, it packs far more flavor per inch and is easier to work with because of the moisture from the eggs. Generally speaking, pasta is easy to make at home; the only time-consuming element is rolling out the dough. Skip weight training in the morning: if you're using a rolling pin or, like me, a wine bottle, the upper body workout will be enough to make you buff.

3 to 3½ cups all-purpose flour, plus more for rolling out the dough

1 teaspoon kosher salt

4 large eggs

1 tablespoon olive oil

INSTRUCTIONS In a large bowl, mix 3 cups of the flour and the salt. Shape a deep well in the middle of the flour; it should look like a white volcano. In another bowl, beat the eggs, then beat in the oil. Slowly pour the egg mixture into the center of the flour, stirring it into the flour. Keep incorporating the eggs into the flour until the mixture gets too stiff to mix with a fork. Switch to your hands and add enough flour, 1 tablespoon at a time, to mix it together into a sticky dough.

Once your dough has come together, turn it out onto a well-floured work surface. Work the dough by pushing the sides into the middle, then bringing the bottom over the top and down, in a repetitive motion. With a steady flow of motion, this should take 8 to 10 minutes of kneading. You'll know it's ready when the dough feels somewhat elastic and it no longer cracks and crumbles while being handled. It will also take on a bit of a subtle shine.

Dampen a clean kitchen towel and wrap the dough in the towel. Let it sit at room temperature for 30 minutes.

Unwrap the dough and, with a scraper or a knife, cut it into equal quarters. Roll the first piece into a ball, flatten it with your hands, then roll it out into a 12-inch square about ⅛ inch thick, keeping the work surface and rolling pin well floured. Repeat with the other pieces of dough. At this point, you're ready to make lasagne (page 50), tagliatelle (page 51), or ravioli (page 47).

HOW TO STORE IT Pasta dough can be stored, wrapped in a damp kitchen towel at room temperature, up to a day. Make sure the towel doesn't dry out.

simple tomato sauce

Makes 3 1/2 cups

TIME COMMITMENT
30 minutes

Put down that jar! This take on the classic pasta sauce is fast and simple, and a great weeknight staple for any kind of pasta, fresh or boxed. It's quick enough to throw together while the water is boiling and extremely versatile. The best way to transform a simple tomato sauce from good to great is to buy the best possible brand of canned tomatoes. Look for canned whole tomatoes from San Marzano—the region of Italy where the most flavorful tomatoes are thought to grow, beloved for their sweet taste and low acidity. You can usually find them at Italian markets or high-end food stores. I favor Italbrand peeled tomatoes for their price and flavor.

PREP AHEAD If you're planning on giving the gift of dried pasta, a jar of this sauce would make an excellent accompaniment. Make sure the jar is free of rust and odors and the lid seals tightly. Prepare a label that lists the contents and date prepared.

1/4 cup olive oil

1 large yellow onion, sliced very thinly

4 cloves garlic, sliced very thinly

3 anchovy fillets (optional)

1 teaspoon dried chile flakes (optional)

1 cup dry red table wine

1 large (28-ounce) can whole Italian tomatoes, with juice

2 teaspoons kosher salt

Freshly ground black pepper

INSTRUCTIONS Heat a sauté pan over medium-high heat. Add the oil and the onion and cook for 6 to 8 minutes, stirring occasionally, until translucent. Add the garlic, plus the anchovies and chile flakes if desired. Stir occasionally, and cook for another 2 minutes. Pour in the wine. While it's bubbling, add the tomatoes by hand 1 at a time, squeezing each whole tomato over the pan to break it up, then dropping the pieces into the pan. (Note that you might want an apron for this job.) Add any remaining juices from the can. Once all the tomatoes have been added, stir the sauce and let it bubble, uncovered, for about 15 minutes, or until thickened. Season to taste with salt and pepper.

HOW TO STORE IT Refrigerate, covered, up to 1 week. Alternatively, this can be kept frozen up to 6 months.

meat, cheese, and spinach filling

Makes 5 cups

TIME COMMITMENT
1 hour

Versatile and colorful, this easy-to-prepare pasta filling can be prepared in advance to give its flavors a chance to come together. It's great for ravioli making (see page 47), since it's easy to handle when cold, and well suited for making lasagne (see page 50), as it can hold its own when sandwiched between sheets of pasta. Prepare the filling before you roll your pasta to give it a chance to cool completely before using.

1½ pounds fresh spinach, stemmed and washed, or 10 ounces frozen

2 tablespoons olive oil

1 yellow onion, chopped

2 tablespoons kosher salt, divided, plus extra as needed

3 cloves garlic, sliced

1 pound lean ground beef

2 teaspoons dried oregano

1 teaspoon dried sage

1 teaspoon fennel seeds, crushed

1 teaspoon dried chile flakes (optional)

2 cups Ricotta Cheese (page 80)

2 tablespoons chopped fresh basil or parsley

1 teaspoon freshly squeezed lemon juice

Freshly ground black pepper

INSTRUCTIONS First, cook the spinach—you may need to do this in batches. Fill a microwave-safe bowl with the spinach, whether fresh or frozen. Sprinkle fresh spinach with water, if using. Heat on high for 1 minute. Stir well, and cook for an additional minute if necessary. Drain the spinach, and squeeze out as much moisture as possible. If using fresh spinach, chop finely. Set aside.

In a large skillet, heat the olive oil over medium-high heat and cook the onion with 1 tablespoon of the salt for 6 to 8 minutes, until translucent. Add the garlic and cook for 1 minute longer. Pour the onions and garlic into another bowl and set aside.

In that same unwashed pan, cook the meat with the remaining 1 tablespoon salt for 5 to 7 minutes, breaking it up with a spoon and scraping up any bits of onion that might be stuck to the bottom, until the meat is browned. Drain off any excess fat. Stir in the oregano, sage, fennel seed, and chile flakes if you like. Return the onions and garlic to the pan, and add the spinach. Stir to combine, and continue to cook for 3 minutes more to let the spinach dry out. Turn off the heat and fold in the cheese. Add the basil and lemon juice. Taste for seasoning and adjust as needed. Allow to cool to room temperature before filling fresh pasta.

HOW TO STORE IT Refrigerate, covered, up to 5 days.

ravioli

Makes about 40 ravioli, or about 4 to 6 servings

TIME COMMITMENT
1 day

Oh, ravioli can be so much better than the stuff that was made famous by a certain Boyardee. Ravioli is the ultimate convenience meal—it cooks fast and can be served simply tossed with butter or tossed with anything imaginable for a fancy dinner. Rather than buying bag upon bag of ready-made limp pouches of ravioli, crafting your own is a satisfying project with delectable results.

5 cups Meat, Cheese, and Spinach Filling (page 46)

1 large egg

1 tablespoon water

4 (12 by 12-inch) sheets Basic Pasta Dough (page 44)

1/4 cup salt

31/2 cups Simple Tomato Sauce (page 45)

Grated Parmesan cheese, for garnish

INSTRUCTIONS Have the filling ready in a bowl and cool enough to handle. In another bowl, beat the egg with the water, and have a pastry brush standing by.

Working with 1 pasta sheet at a time, brush the entire sheet with the egg wash, and cut off the edges to make it into a perfect square. Measure out with a ruler (or eyeball) the middle of the pasta sheet, and mark it with a slight indentation of your finger. Drop teaspoonfuls of filling onto one-half of the pasta sheet, leaving at least a 1/2-inch border, and at least 1 inch between them. There should be room for 15 spoonfuls of filling.

Carefully fold the pasta sheet in half over the filling. Gently press out as much air as you can around each ball of filling. Next, gently press a separation between each row and each column of ravioli. Once you feel confident

// CONTINUED

ravioli, CONTINUED

that each raviolo has the right shape, press the dough firmly into shape. Carefully cut out each row, then each column, using a pizza cutter, scraper, or knife. Once each raviolo has been cut out, pinch it firmly around all 4 sides. Repeat this process for the remaining 3 sheets of pasta, moving finished ravioli to a well-floured rimmed baking sheet.

Let the ravioli air-dry for at least 30 minutes. To cook, boil a large stockpot of water with the salt. Once it has achieved a rapid boil, gently add the pasta and stir. Start tasting the pasta after 9 minutes. Cooking time will vary, depending on the size of the ravioli. Note that some may also be done more quickly than others; remove smaller ones from the pot as needed. The largest ravioli should not take more than 15 minutes.

While the ravioli are cooking, heat the sauce. Once fully cooked, drain the ravioli and toss with the sauce. Garnish with the cheese.

HOW TO STORE IT For long-term storage, let the ravioli air-dry for at least 30 minutes to allow a good seal to form, place in the freezer, and freeze for at least 4 hours. Once fully frozen, transfer the ravioli to a sealable plastic bag, marked with the contents and date prepared. These will last in the freezer up to 6 months.

lasagne

Makes 1 (9 by 13-inch) lasagne, or about 9 to 12 servings

TIME COMMITMENT
1 day

This version of lasagne features several food groups from The Delicious Pyramid—meat, cheese, tangy tomato, and tender noodle. I'm always amazed by how many home cooks sweat over their secret lasagne sauce and lovingly chop meat and grill vegetables for the filling, but when it comes to the actual pasta—the foundation of the dish—they reach for a cardboard box of flavorless noodles. Lasagne made of fresh pasta is one of the easiest noodle dishes to prepare at home.

4 (12 by 12-inch) sheets Basic Pasta Dough (page 44)

5 cups Simple Tomato Sauce (page 45)

5 cups Meat, Cheese, and Spinach Filling (page 46)

1 pound mozzarella cheese, shredded or thinly sliced

INSTRUCTIONS Preheat the oven to 350°F.

With a knife, scraper, or pizza cutter, slice each pasta sheet into 2- to 3-inch-wide noodles. Note that some noodles cut from the center will have long, straight edges on both sides, and that those cut from the ends will be slightly curved.

To assemble the lasagne, in the bottom of a 9 by 13-inch baking dish, spread 1 generous cup of tomato sauce. Lay the long, rectangular noodles across the bottom. Choose noodles with long, straight edges for both edges of the pan, and reserve the awkwardly shaped, slightly rounded noodles for the interior. Cut the noodles to fit the space, making sure the noodles go all the way to the edge. Save any unused scraps. Let the noodles overlap one another slightly and use the scraps to fill in any gaps, so that the entire bottom of the dish is covered. Evenly distribute 1 1/2 cups of the meat filling in tablespoonfuls over the top of the pasta. Note that the filling won't spread, so just drop it onto the pasta. Next, add a thin layer using one-quarter of the cheese.

Spoon another generous cup of tomato sauce evenly over the top. Layer the next sheet of pasta as before. Once that second layer is complete, gently press down on the pasta to lightly flatten and compress the layers of the dish.

Repeat the layering of 1 1/2 cups of meat filling, one-quarter of the mozarella, a rounded cup of the tomato sauce, and another sheet of pasta. Repeat again. Reserve one-quarter of the mozzarella. Once the final sheet of pasta has been added, press into the lasagne gently to "set" the ingredients in place. Cover the top pasta sheet with 1 1/2 cups of the tomato sauce. You will end up with 4 layers of pasta and 3 layers of meat, topped with sauce.

To finish the dish, cover tightly with aluminum foil and bake for 40 minutes. Remove the foil and scatter the last of the cheese evenly over the top. Bake for an additional 20 to 30 minutes, or until brown and bubbly.

HOW TO STORE IT The lasagne can be assembled and refrigerated, covered, a day ahead. Once cooked, it can be kept refrigerated up to 1 week. To freeze, cook covered for just 30 minutes and allow it to come to room temperature. Add the cheese to the top and refrigerate until cold, at least 6 hours, wrap tightly with two layers of foil, then freeze. It will keep frozen up to 2 months.

tagliatelle

Makes about 1 pound,
or about 6 servings

TIME COMMITMENT
1 day

When we think about pasta for dinner, the first image that comes to mind is a plate of long, thin noodles waiting to be wound around the tines of a fork. *Tagliatelle* is that quintessential Italian dish: long noodles approximately 1/4 to 3/4 inch wide. Of course, if your patience and your knife skills allow it, you can slice the noodles thinner to make *capellini*, or wider for *pappardelle*. No matter what you call them, you will have ribbons of homemade pasta with excellent texture and real flavor, ready to receive the sauce of your choice.

4 (12 by 12-inch) sheets Basic Pasta Dough (page 44)
1/4 cup kosher salt
3 1/2 cups Simple Tomato Sauce (page 45)
Grated Parmesan cheese, for garnish

INSTRUCTIONS Working with 1 pasta sheet at a time, flour the sheet well, then gently fold the dough in thirds (like a letter), for easier cutting. Use a pizza cutter, knife, or metal dough scraper to cut the dough into long strips, about 1/4 to 3/4 inch wide. Cut it as wide or as thin as you'd like; the most important thing is that you try to be consistent throughout for more even cooking later.

Flour a large rimmed baking sheet well. Once all the pasta has been cut, gently unfold each strand and let it rest, stretched long, on the baking sheet to dry. Cut the 3 remaining sheets of pasta as above, allowing them to dry slightly as well.

To cook the pasta, boil a large stockpot of water with the salt. Once it has achieved a rapid boil, gently add the pasta and stir. Start tasting the pasta after 5 to 7 minutes; it should be soft throughout and visibly cooked in the middle. Cooking time will vary with the size of the noodles. If they are on the large side, it could take as long as 12 minutes.

While you're cooking the pasta, heat the sauce. Drain the pasta well and toss with the sauce. Garnish with the cheese.

HOW TO STORE IT Storing fresh pasta is a rewarding task: simply find a place in your home to hang the pasta and let it air-dry overnight or for about 8 hours. I usually balance a clean oven rack over 2 large mixing bowls and lay the pasta, strand by strand, over the rack. Once dried, move the pasta to sealable plastic bags, date it, and shelve it up to a year. To cook dried pasta, follow the instructions above, but add an extra 3 to 5 minutes to the cooking time.

5 | hook it

PRESERVED AND CURED FISH

Preserved fish is a thing of great beauty. Even those who turn up their noses at the sight, smell, and general slipperiness of fresh fish may have difficulty keeping their fins away from the finished product atop a perfect chewy bagel and a smear of cream cheese. Smoked, salted, and cured fish usually requires a trip to a Scandinavian market or Jewish deli, but it needn't be such an effort.

Lots of salt, some smoke, and a critter of the sea are all you need to easily throw together your own appetizing deli counter with minimal effort. Salt, one of the oldest and tried-and-true preservatives, is the key ingredient that simultaneously slows spoilage, adds flavor, and draws out moisture. Smoke is an equally ancient and effective natural preservative, adding the flavor of the grill and desiccating the liquid from the meat. Both yield results that are delicious, mind-bendingly easy, and entirely worth your time.

Your friends will come to your place for brunch hook, line, and sinker, and with these recipes, you can afford to feed them. Serve the fish on bagels, or pair with crackers or flatbread (page 5) and some homemade yogurt cheese (page 78).

gravlax

Makes about 3/4 pound

TIME COMMITMENT
3 days

What's the difference between gravlax and smoked salmon? Gravlax is made by curing fish in salt, sugar, and spice while tightly wrapped, following the traditional Scandinavian method. Smoked salmon, its eastern European cousin, is a cold smoked fish with terrific smoky flavor. For those of us living in tight quarters and with barely enough room for a small BBQ, cold-smoking just ain't gonna happen. This simple recipe for gravlax, however, will certainly satisfy that pang for thin-sliced, briny, cured seafood. Serve on bread with homemade mustard sauce (page 26), a squeeze of fresh lemon juice, fresh dill sprigs, capers, and thinly sliced red onion for the full cured-fish experience.

---

1 pound best-quality, freshest salmon you can find

3 tablespoons kosher salt

3 tablespoons sugar

2 teaspoons freshly ground black pepper

1 large bunch fresh dill, stems trimmed

INSTRUCTIONS Pat the salmon dry. In a small bowl, mix the salt and sugar. Cut the length of the salmon in half, and rub the mixture into each piece generously on all 4 sides, including the skin. Place 1 fillet atop 2 generous sheets of plastic wrap, skin side down. Sprinkle with 1 teaspoon of the black pepper, and spread one-half of the dill around all the exposed fleshy parts of the fish. Wrap with 1 layer of plastic wrap, trying to secure the position of the dill. Wrap tightly with another layer of plastic. Repeat with the second piece of salmon.

Put both wrapped pieces in a small dish capable of retaining any liquids that might be released during the cure. Store, dill side up, in the fridge for 3 days. Unwrap, discard the dill, rinse off any remaining solids, and pat dry again.

To serve, slice long, thin pieces on a lateral bias with a very sharp knife.

HOW TO STORE IT Refrigerate, wrapped tightly in plastic wrap, up to 2 weeks.

VARIATION In addition to the dill, add 1/2 cup sliced fresh fennel bulb, 2 tablespoons cumin seeds, or several long strips of orange zest (from about half an orange) to the fish before tightly wrapping it in plastic.

salt cod

Makes about 1/2 to
3/4 pound

TIME COMMITMENT
4 to 5 days

Salted and air-cured cod is a frequent star on the inland menus of Portugal, Italy, and France, for good reason. It stores well and travels easily, and its mild fish flavor lends itself to a number of dishes and appetizers. While it may seem absurd to cure and dry fish just to reconstitute it later, the curing process completely transforms the flavor and texture of the cod—think cucumbers versus pickles. Note that salt cod cannot be eaten as is: once dried, it requires 24 to 36 hours of soaking in 4 to 5 changes of water to bring the flesh back to life. Also note that it must be cooked—trendy recipes du jour include European classics like *brandade*, a mash of the fish with cream and potatoes, and fried salt cod fritters. As Atlantic Cod is terribly overfished, I strongly recommend using Pacific Cod— also called Alaska Cod, True Cod, or Grey Cod—for this recipe. Look for fish that is 1/2 to 3/4 inch thick.

1 pound cod, bones and skin removed
Kosher salt

INSTRUCTIONS Lay the fish in the center of a clean kitchen towel and cover completely with salt, about 1/4 to 1/2 cup on 1 side. Flip the fish, and cover the other side with salt as well, rubbing on enough to cover the sides of the fish. Wrap the fish in the towel and lay it on a rack over a baking dish. Refrigerate for 10 to 12 hours; the towel should be quite wet, and the fish will decrease in volume. Salt and wrap again with a clean towel, and refrigerate for another 10 to 12 hours.

The fish should feel firm and rigid around its thinner edges, a sign that it is beginning to cure. Put the fish back on the rack, this time without any cover. Rub it with more salt on its thickest parts, as much as will cling to the bottom and just enough to cover the top. Flip the fish twice a day, adding a light sprinkling of salt, 1 teaspoon or so, until it is firm and resistant to touch throughout. Let it dry out like this in the refrigerator for 2 to 3 days, flipping it twice daily. The fish is cured when it is firm and rigid to the touch all over. Time to completion will vary depending on the thickness of the fish.

HOW TO STORE IT Wrap in waxed paper and double-bag in sealable plastic bags. Refrigerate the fish, covered, up to 4 months.

smoked trout

Makes 3/4 pound

TIME COMMITMENT
About 2 hours

This fish is one of the easiest and fastest to smoke at home. Beware, you may become addicted to it. Smoked trout makes terrific hors d'oeuvres on crackers (page 5) with crème fraîche and a sprig of green chive or dill. You can also flake the fish or put it in a food processor with 1/2 cup mayonnaise to make a delicious fish dip. Make sure you have some hickory sawdust (available at www.sausagemaker.com) on hand for smoking, as well as a meat thermometer, which is the best test to know if the fish is done.

PREP AHEAD Have 2 cups of hickory sawdust on hand.

1 tablespoon kosher salt
1 tablespoon golden brown sugar
2 (8-ounce) boneless trout

INSTRUCTIONS In a small bowl, combine the salt and sugar with your fingers. Use paper towels to dry off the fish as much as possible. Cover a plate with more clean paper towels, put the fish on top, and rub, inside and out, with the salt and sugar mixture. Allow the fish to sit at room temperature for 30 minutes. It will release a good amount of moisture. Try to drain as much moisture from the fish as possible before laying it on the grill.

Meanwhile, prepare the grill by cleaning it and lighting the charcoal, if necessary (see page 60). Prepare the packet of hickory sawdust (see page 60).

When the coals are ready (covered with gray ash, with no red glowing parts), push them to 1 side of the grill and set the packet of sawdust on top of them (if you are using a gas grill, put the packet on the lava rocks or grill plate on the hot side of the grill). Place the fish on the "cool" side of the grill, opposite the coals or the lit burner. Close down the lid, making sure the vents over the fish are open, and smoke for 1 hour, then flip and rotate the fish. Smoke for another 30 minutes, then insert a thermometer into both fish. When they've reached 140°F, they are fully cooked.

Note that you may need a second batch of coals after 1 1/2 hours. Open the grill lid as infrequently as possible to keep the heat and smoke inside. When you flip and rotate the fish, take the opportunity to also check if the coals are still hot enough by holding your hand a few inches above the grill rack. If you can hold it there comfortably for about 6 seconds, the coals are still hot enough.

Allow the fish to cool to room temperature.

HOW TO STORE IT Refrigerate, wrapped in plastic, up to 10 days.

6 | hunt it

PRESERVED AND CURED MEAT

Call your butcher and make him or her your friend, as you're going to be spending time together. Why? Most of the meats and animal parts called for in the recipes that follow will likely need to be special-ordered from your favorite meat source. Life is too short for factory-farmed slop meat. If you're going to put forth the effort to brine, grind, and smoke it, be sure to use top-quality, grass-fed critters.

Handcrafting your own meat is one of the most satisfying kitchen projects there is: it's not terribly difficult, just a little time-consuming, and it's incredibly impressive. People are flabbergasted when you tell them that you've created what their steak knife is digging into. The best part is that it allows you to control the quality of the meat you are serving and skip the additives and chemical ingredients that are all too common in the mass-market versions. The result is a far superior product to what you can find at the grocery store—and for a lot less moola. So grab your chef's knife, a spear, and your testosterone. It's time to meet your meat.

HOW TO SMOKE ON THE GRILL

Here's what you'll need to make smoking magic happen:

A grill in good working order. Your grill should be free of large piles of ash at the bottom. Open the vents on the bottom and the top for smoking. Use a heavy-duty wire brush to clean the rack between uses.

Charcoal. Look for 100 percent natural hardwood. Note that you'll pay more for those that have very large (and slow-burning) pieces. While the cheaper stuff works too, the pieces are smaller, meaning you'll be burning through it faster and your fire will need more babysitting.

Hickory sawdust. Though sawdust is more difficult to find than wood chips, it does not require presoaking. If you can't find it, order it at www.sausagemaker.com.

Meat thermometer. This gauge is the only sure way to test for readiness. Fish is ready when it reaches 140°F, meat 150°F, and poultry 160°F.

Prepare your grill. If you are cooking with charcoal, it's best to use either a chimney starter or an electric starter (don't use lighter fluid or your food will taste like lighter fluid). If you are using a chimney starter, crumple up a few sheets of newspaper at the bottom of the chimney starter, then pile charcoal on top. Place the chimney starter on the bottom rack of the grill and light the paper. Once all the charcoal is alight and red-hot, carefully pour the charcoal out of the starter, and add more charcoal as desired. If you are using an electric starter, make a pyramid of about 5 or 6 cups of charcoal on the bottom grill rack, insert the starter's loop into the middle of the pyramid, and plug it in. Remove the starter once the charcoal is ignited.

To smoke-cook foods, you want a low heat. With a gas grill, you'll want one burner turned on at the low setting. For charcoal, this means all of your coals should be covered with gray ash, with no red glow.

While your coals are heating, tear off two (18- to 20-inch) long pieces of aluminum foil and lay them on top of each other on a flat surface. Fill the inside of the foil with 4 or 5 cups of the hickory sawdust. Wrap the foil around the sawdust into a flat package, ensuring that all of it is contained inside. Flip the packet over and poke 10 to 12 holes on the top of the package. This foil pack will keep the sawdust from burning too quickly, and it will help to produce some flavorful smoke. Note that if you have wood chips rather than sawdust, you should soak them in water to cover for about 30 minutes, then drain them before wrapping them in foil.

Once the coals are ready, transfer them to one side of the grill. Placement is important; if the meat is too close to the heat, it will grill, rather than smoke. Place the foil pack, hole side up, directly on top of the coals. If you are using a gas grill, put the foil pack on the lava rocks or grill plate on the hot side of the grill.

Place your meat on the cold side of the grill (opposite the coals or the lit burner), with the thickest piece closest to the heat, skin side up. Cover the grill and make sure that the open vents are over the meat, thus guiding the smoke to pass over the meat as it escapes. For smoking, the lid should always be on (except when checking for doneness or adding more coals). There should always be a trickle of smoke coming out from the upper vents.

You'll need new coals after about 2 hours of smoking, which means you may need to light a new batch after $1\frac{1}{2}$ hours if you're smoking something that takes more than 2 hours. A new foil pack of sawdust may be necessary if you're smoking for more than 4 hours. Have your meat thermometer standing by, and always test for temperature in the thickest part of the flesh.

smoked turkey

Makes about 1 1/2 pounds

TIME COMMITMENT
About 2 days

Ever wonder what makes turkey sandwiches—and I don't mean those post-Thanksgiving leftover suckers, but the deli counter variety you gobble down at lunch—insanely addictive? It's the robust smoke in the turkey that gives it its distinctive flavor and its character. Although bone-in turkey is perfectly easy to find during the holiday months, you might need to call your butcher ahead of time to make sure they have it in stock the rest of the year. Because temperature is the only way to truly know if a piece of smoked meat is cooked all the way through, make sure you have a meat thermometer handy.

PREP AHEAD Have 4 cups of hickory sawdust on hand.

- 8 cups water
- 1/2 cup kosher salt
- 2 tablespoons sugar
- 5 cloves garlic, smashed
- 2 tablespoons peppercorns
- 3 to 4 sprigs fresh basil, rosemary, or thyme
- 1 (2 1/2-pound) bone-in, skin-on turkey breast

INSTRUCTIONS In a large bowl, make a brine by combining the water, salt, sugar, garlic, peppercorns, and basil and mixing to dissolve the salt and sugar. Submerge the turkey in the brine completely, even if you need to add more water to do so. Weight the bird with an inverted dinner plate to keep it covered. Place in the refrigerator, and let sit for 24 hours.

Discard the brine and all the solid ingredients, and rinse the turkey. Pat it dry and let it sit in the refrigerator, uncovered, for 2 hours.

Meanwhile, prepare the grill by cleaning it and lighting the charcoal, if necessary (see page 60). Prepare the packet of hickory sawdust (see page 60).

When the coals are ready (covered with gray ash, with no red glowing parts), push them to one side of the grill and set the packet of sawdust on top of them (if you are using a gas grill, put the packet on the lava rocks or grill plate on the hot side of the grill). Place the turkey on the "cool" side of the grill, opposite the coals or the lit burner. Close down the lid and smoke the turkey skin side up, with the thickest portion closest to the flame, for 1 1/2 to 2 1/2 hours, until its interior temperature reaches 160°F. Note that you may need a second batch of coals after 1 1/2 hours. Open the grill lid as infrequently as possible to keep the heat and smoke inside. When you check the internal temperature of the meat, take the opportunity to also check if the coals are still hot enough by holding your hand a few inches above the grill rack. If you can hold it there comfortably for about 6 seconds, the temperature is still hot enough.

HOW TO STORE IT Once the turkey is cooked and cooled, discard the skin and bone and slice the meat into sandwich-ready slices. Refrigerate, wrapped tightly in plastic wrap or in an airtight container, up to 1 week.

bacon

Nothing could be simpler than makin' bacon, the king of all fried meats. How many "vegetarians" have you known who just eat the periodic slab of crisp sautéed hog fat? I rest my case. Bacon is God. To cure your own bacon, plan and shop for ingredients well in advance. You might need to special-order the pork belly from your local butcher or grocery store. You can order curing salt from online retailers such as www.sausagemaker .com; I recommend Insta-Cure #1. In this recipe, I offer three ways to smoke the bacon. If you go the liquid smoke route, use only the real stuff: fake liquid smoke has an unappealing chemical taste. If you choose to smoke the meat on the grill, you'll need some hickory sawdust, which is available in smoking stores or through online retailers. Once the bacon is ready to eat, note that it will be easiest to slice thinly—a must if you like crispy bacon—when it is partially frozen and your knife is very sharp.

PREP AHEAD Have on hand 3 tablespoons of real liquid hickory smoke or 5 cups of hickory sawdust, depending on the method you've chosen to smoke the bacon.

2 1/2 to 3 pounds pork belly

1/2 cup sugar

1 tablespoon blackstrap molasses

2 tablespoons kosher salt, plus more as needed

1 teaspoon curing salt

1 teaspoon freshly ground black pepper

INSTRUCTIONS Rinse the belly and thoroughly pat it dry. Trim off any thin edges so that the piece is one long rectangle. (You can save these excess pieces of belly for making sausage or lard.)

In a small bowl, mix the sugar with the molasses. Then mix in the 2 tablespoons of salt, curing salt, and pepper and rub it evenly into the meat (like a relaxing, porcine spa treatment). Place the meat inside an oversize sealable plastic bag and lay it flat in the refrigerator for 7 days, massaging the liquids that will amass through the bag and flipping it daily.

After 7 days, inspect your bacon. It should be firm to the touch all over, like touching a cooked steak—a sign that it has been cured. If the flesh still feels spongy and soft in spots, massage the meat again with an additional 2 tablespoons salt and check it again after 1 or 2 days.

Once the bacon is fully cured, discard the solids, rinse the meat well, and pat it dry.

The next step to giving bacon that familiar flavor is the addition of smoke.

Fastest: Roasting and Liquid Smoke Preheat the oven to 200°F. Place the belly, fat side up, on a rack over a roasting pan and roast for 2 to 2 1/2 hours, until the interior temperature of the meat reaches 150°F.

// CONTINUED

Gently brush the liquid smoke over the entirety of the bacon, covering both sides evenly.

Slowest: Smoking on the Grill Refer to "How to Smoke," page 60. Smoke the meat, fat side up, using a 5-cup packet of hickory sawdust, for 3 to 5 hours, until it reaches an internal temperature of 150°F.

Best of Both Worlds: Smoking and Roasting This is my preferred methodology, because I love the flavor of the smoke but often lack the patience for a full grill session. Start smoking your meat, and do so as long as you're able—at least 2 hours is really ideal. Smoke it until you get sick of babysitting the grill and tending to the coals. Finish the meat on a rack over a roasting pan in a 200°F oven until it reaches 150°F inside at its thickest point.

Fry a slice of the bacon and taste. If it needs more smoke flavor, brush a thin layer of liquid smoke on both sides of the slab.

Whichever method you use, when your bacon is ready, slice it as thin (or as thick) as you like it and fry, over medium-high heat, until browned on both sides. Drain on paper towels and enjoy.

HOW TO STORE IT Bacon can be stored in large slabs, in precut hunks for flavoring beans or other dishes, or in slices, in layers between pieces of parchment paper, and sealed tightly in a freezer storage bag. Refrigerate up to 10 days or keep frozen up to 3 months.

lard

Makes 4 to 5 cups

TIME COMMITMENT
2 days

Homemade lard is an amazing culinary fat with a rich flavor and a very high smoking point—and unlike the shelf-stable variety, it does not contain partially hydrogenated anything. Though it may seem a bit extreme to render your own pork fat, it is fun and eminently satisfying, lending a taste of country bumpkinness to our busy urban existence. In addition to being perfect for making pie crusts, this will be your preferred fat for pan-frying almost everything—from meat and fish to vegetables and cheese. Like all great meat-based cooking projects, the ultimate product depends on using high-quality, fresh hog fat, which your local butcher shop or sausage maker may have to special-order.

PREP AHEAD You'll need clean jars to store the lard. Make sure they are free of rust and odors and the lids seal tightly. Prepare a label that lists the contents and date prepared.

2^1/$_2$ to 3 pounds pork fatback
3 cups water, divided

INSTRUCTIONS Remove as many trace elements of meat, tissue, and skin as you can and chop the fat, roughly into 2-inch cubes. Be careful while handling your knife, because the fat can leave your hands slippery.

Move the fatback to a heavy-bottomed pot (cast iron is best) with a lid, and stir in 1 cup of the water. Turn the heat to medium-low and cover. Stir occasionally, making sure the fat isn't sticking to the bottom of the pot. Allow it to melt down, and the water to evaporate, for 5 to 6 hours. Keep the heat low; it should emit only the occasional bubble but not simmer.

You'll notice that your fatback is getting brown and sticky, and it looks as if the pieces are no longer melt-ing down. When this happens, turn off the heat, let it cool slightly, and scrape up as much as you can from the bottom and sides of the pot. Carefully pour the lard through a sieve into a very large bowl. Press down on the solids to extract as much fat from them as possible. (Incidentally, these solid pieces remaining in the sieve are a delicious snack unto themselves. Serve cracklings on toast with a sprinkle of salt and you have a poor man's pâté.)

Don't worry if the lard is brown; it will turn white when it cools. Mix the warm lard with the remaining 2 cups of water, cover the bowl, and refrigerate overnight or for 6 to 8 hours.

Scoop out the lard, and discard the water and all of its debris. Try to keep the lard clean by removing any other clinging brown bits.

Melt the finished lard in a clean pot, then pour into glass jars.

HOW TO STORE IT Refrigerate, covered, for at least 4 months, or keep frozen up to 1 year.

sausage patties

Grinding sausage is its own reward that will yield meat for breakfast or for dinner for months to come. Its bright fresh flavors, rarely matched by any store-bought sausage, come from using the best meat you can find. Check with your butcher before heading to the market, since fatback—also called back fat—may need to be special-ordered. Note that fatback should not have any skin on it. If it does, remove it before cooking with it. Also, make sure that you're buying just fat and not salt pork: they look alike, but the latter will render your finished product almost inedible from saltiness. And most important, you can't make low-fat sausage, so don't skimp on the fatback.

PREP AHEAD You'll need a meat grinder, either a sturdy metal monster that clamps on to the kitchen counter or the fancy attachment that connects to an electric stand mixer.

2 pounds cold pork butt or shoulder, cut into long strips 2 inches wide

8 ounces cold, hard pork fatback, cut into 1- to 2-inch strips

3 cloves garlic, minced

1 tablespoon dried fennel

1 teaspoon dried rosemary

1 teaspoon dried sage

1 to 2 tablespoons kosher salt

Freshly ground black pepper

1 teaspoon dried chile flakes

2 tablespoons freshly squeezed lemon juice

INSTRUCTIONS Make certain that both the meat and the fat are very cold by refrigerating them for 6 hours or putting them in the freezer for 30 minutes. Grind them in tandem, alternating between the meat and the fat, using the large-holed plate of your meat grinder. If you desire a smoother texture to your sausage, chill the meat for 30 minutes and grind again, this time using the small-holed plate of the grinder.

In a large bowl, use your hands to combine the ground meat and fat with the garlic, fennel, rosemary, sage, salt, pepper, chile flakes, and lemon juice.

Heat a small frying pan on medium-high heat and make a small patty from 2 teaspoons of the meat. Fry the miniature patty, then taste for seasoning and adjust as needed. Do not skip this step: it's important to make sure the sausage has a good flavor before moving forward.

Spoon the meat into your hand, 2 tablespoons at a time, and pat it into a circular patty about 1/4 inch thick, placing on a rimmed baking sheet. When all the patties are formed, fry in an ungreased skillet over medium-high heat for 3 minutes, until very brown. Flip and fry on the second side until very brown, another 2 or 3 minutes. Drain on paper towels and devour.

HOW TO STORE IT Line a large, airtight container with waxed paper or parchment paper. Place each patty in the container in a single layer, and don't allow the patties to touch. Layer additional patties on top between sheets of waxed paper or parchment paper. Refrigerate, covered, up to 1 week. For long-term storage, place formed but not cooked patties on a waxed paper–lined rimmed baking sheet with patties close, but not touching. Freeze for 2 hours, then move frozen patties to an airtight container or sealable plastic bag. Prepare a label that lists the contents and date prepared. Store in the freezer up to 4 months.

VARIATIONS For a fruitier sausage, add 2 tablespoons fresh orange zest and substitute orange juice for the lemon juice. For a hot and sweet sausage, increase the chile flakes to 2 teaspoons and add 2 tablespoons honey. For a more savory sausage, mix 5 chopped anchovies in with the meat and the other ingredients.

sausage links

Makes about 10 links

TIME COMMITMENT
3 to 4 hours

Preparing your own sausage links is the ultimate in culinary home improvement. They say that homemade sausage links are a "gateway" meat, leading to an insatiable lust for homemade pancetta and *lardo*, and an endless pursuit of quality *salumi*. Before you know it, you'll be moving the clothes out of the closet to make room for a humidifier and to hang cured and cased meat. This new hobby of yours has a learning curve, however. Stuffing sausage is definitely something you have to get the knack of, and it's likely that your later sets of links will look more uniform and consistent than your first. Both, however, are equally edible. Sausage links require casings, available at some butcher shops and markets, or online at www.sausagemaker.com. I like the 1 1/4- to 1 3/8-inch hog casings, as they're sturdy and the right thickness for a regular Italian-style sausage that can be eaten on a bun or not. Casings are usually sold by the pound, and this will be more than enough for any home cook. They will last in the fridge for at least a year.

PREP AHEAD You'll need a meat grinder, either a sturdy metal monster that clamps on to the kitchen counter or the fancy attachment that connects to an electric stand mixer, as well as an attachment for stuffing sausages (usually sold separately). Make certain that you have a large wooden spoon to push the meat into the grinder, and a large rimmed baking sheet to hold the finished links.

3 3/4 cups cold sausage meat (page 68)
2 (48-inch) pieces hog casings
2 tablespoons neutral vegetable oil, like canola or sunflower
1 cup water, wine, or stock

INSTRUCTIONS Beginners should be sure to read this process all the way through before launching into stuffing. And it may be helpful to have a kitchen assistant standing by. Keep your fully prepared sausage meat cold until you're ready to start stuffing.

Cut the hog casings from the package, and pull one end gently over the nozzle of the kitchen faucet. Turn the water on to a slow stream, and with your hands gently guide it through the entire length of the casing, flushing out the interior. Let the water run through each segment for a couple of minutes to clean it out thoroughly. Then allow the casings to hydrate in a bowl of cool tap water for at least 30 minutes.

Add the sausage stuffing hardware to your meat grinder. Now you're ready to stuff. Sheathe the first piece of casing entirely over the nozzle of the sausage stuffer, handling the casing gently to prevent tearing. Keep a towel nearby, and try to soak up as much moisture from the casing as possible. Pull off a "tail" of 4 to 5 inches of casing from the nozzle. Do not knot.

Activate your grinder to medium speed, stuffing the sausage into the combine as you work. You'll likely feel or see a bit of air coming through the cone. Allow all of the air to be expressed. Once you see a solid stream of meat coming out through the cone and into the casing, pause the grinder and make a knot as close to the meat as you can. The goal here is to try to keep as much air out of the finished product as possible. Oh, and don't think of horror movies. Think about how great your homemade sausage is going to taste.

With continued stuffing—and sometimes it's best to have one person stuff the grinder while another person mans the sausage—the meat will come out fast and furious. Work slowly, and guide the meat into the casing, trying to avoid as much air inside as you can. Don't worry about it being perfectly smooth—you can fix the shape later. What's important is to allow each sausage to get rounded and plump—tight, but not bursting. Achieve this by holding the casing briefly in place and letting the meat fill it to capacity, then pulling out the casing a bit more, allowing it to fill. Let each sausage fill to about 5 inches long. Twist the casing several times to provide a break before the next sausage starts to fill. Continue this process until you have a chain of sausages and about 4 inches of empty casing on the other side. Turn off the machine. Take this first set of links off the stuffer, and make a knot on this end as close to the meat as possible. Lay them on the rimmed baking sheet.

Twist each of the breaks between the sausages to ensure that it's tight and that there's about a $1/8$-inch space between each link. Take a few minutes to shape each sausage into a smooth, even link. Marvel at what you've accomplished.

Start the process again with the other piece of casing. Keep working until all of the meat has been cased. You will likely have more casing than you can use, but it's better to have too much than not enough. Discard unused soaked casing.

Let your sausages firm up in the refrigerator for at least 4 to 6 hours or overnight before cooking.

To cook sausages, cut the desired amount of links from the chain using kitchen shears, being careful not to puncture the adjoining sausage. Make some tiny holes along the casing with a toothpick. Heat the oil in a skillet on medium-high heat, and sear the sausages for about 10 minutes, or until browned all over. Once browned, pour in the water, cover, and allow to steam for an additional 5 minutes. If you plan to serve sliced sausages, cook them first, then slice.

HOW TO STORE IT Refrigerate, covered or wrapped in plastic, up to 1 week, or in the freezer in a sealable plastic bag for at least 6 months.

beef jerky

Makes 8 ounces

TIME COMMITMENT
2 days

Once you learn to make this addictive and full-flavored savory snack, you'll never again have a need for that store-bought shoe leather. The key to making beef jerky is slicing the meat very thinly. I recommend asking your butcher to slice the meat against the grain for you when you buy it. If this is not an option, freeze the meat for 30 minutes, then slice with a very sharp knife.

PREP AHEAD Have on hand neutral vegetable oil, like canola or sunflower, to prepare the rack.

- 1 pound very lean top sirloin or flank steak, sliced 1/8 to 1/4 inch thick
- 1 tablespoon kosher salt
- 1 tablespoon soy sauce
- 2 teaspoons dark brown sugar
- 2 cloves garlic, minced
- 1 teaspoon dried chile flakes (optional)
- 1 teaspoon cracked black pepper (optional)

INSTRUCTIONS Using your best surgeon's hand, remove every trace of fat from the meat. Don't skip this step. Meat can be cured, whereas fat cannot. If you leave fat on the meat, it will likely go rancid later on.

Lay all of the meat between 2 clean kitchen towels and press out as much of its moisture as you can. Facilitate this process and help the meat tenderize by pounding it using your favorite implement (a sturdy mug, a hammer, or a meat tenderizer).

In a bowl, toss the meat with the salt, soy sauce, sugar, and garlic with your hands, adding chile flakes and pepper if you wish. Note that the addition of the pepper will give the jerky a nice zing.

Place a rack over a large rimmed baking sheet covered with foil, and rub the rack lightly with oil. Lay the meat over the rack in a single layer, making it as flat as possible, without pieces touching. Refrigerate, uncovered, for 24 hours. This will help marinate the flavor into the meat and shorten the drying process.

Preheat the oven to 150°F, if you can. If your oven can't go lower than 170°F, which is the case with most modern ovens, set it to its lowest temperature and keep the door ajar with a wooden spoon.

Dry the meat in the oven for 3 to 5 hours, checking it for the first time after about 3 hours. The jerky should not be brittle, but it should tear into strings and not look raw inside.

Allow the jerky to cool completely.

HOW TO STORE IT Refrigerate, in a sealable plastic bag, up to 6 weeks.

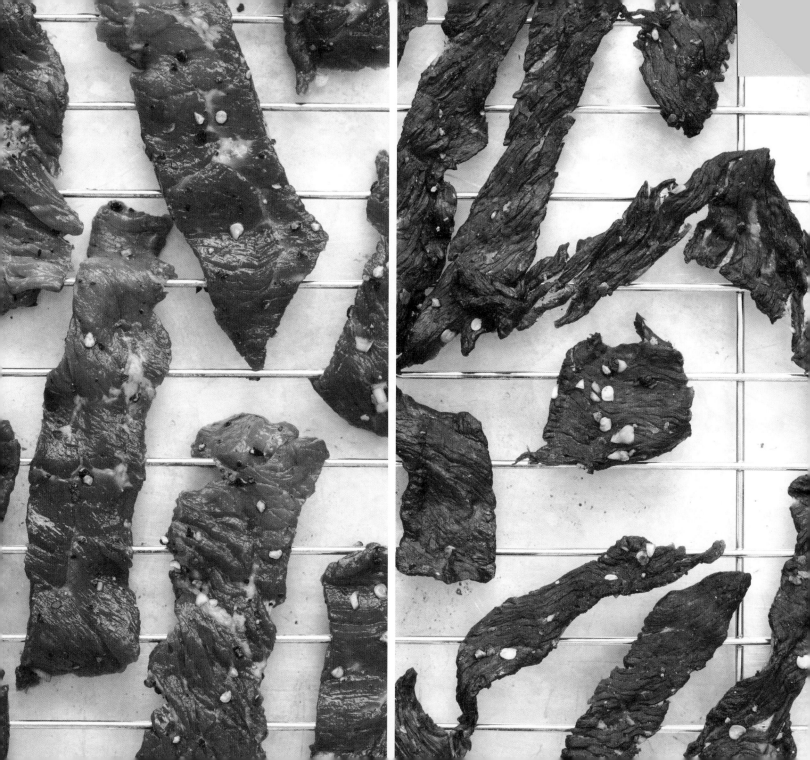

7 | milk it

BUTTER AND CHEESE

Nothing is as important to the craft of making homemade cheese and butter as their main ingredient: milk. For all dairy projects, it's important to use milk or cream that is the freshest and least tampered with that you can find. I'm going to assume that, like me, you don't have access to your own dairy cows and that your milk and cream will come in a carton, rather than a bucket. These recipes will be of use to those using store-bought milk.

When it comes to making curd cheeses, you could use skim or low-fat milk, but nothing compares to the full-mouth flavor of whole milk, which results in a more flavorful final result. Always use pasteurized milk, since the cheese curds will not come together if you use ultra-pasteurized milk, and go for organic, which tastes a whole lot better. The cheeses for which I provide recipes in the pages that follow, while not the most complex or aged, are virtually foolproof, entirely versatile, and require few specialty ingredients. Yet despite their simplicity, they never fail to impress, and making them is a nifty way to spend an afternoon. All of these cheeses, and the butter, are fresh—meaning their flavor will only plummet into mold if you let them sit around for too long. Make them often and eat them right away.

butter

Makes 1/2 to 3/4 cup

TIME COMMITMENT
Less than 2 hours

Remember fourth-grade science class? Take that memory and spread it on toast. The flavor of freshly churned cream will be even better than you remember. Butters or compound butters (a very scientific term that refers to butter that has been mixed with other yummy stuff) can be an elegant component in an edible gift of bread or crackers. Press it into decorative candy molds or paper-lined cupcake tins, or, when the butter is very cold, cut it into shapes with a cookie cutter. Making your own butter also yields a second reward: fresh buttermilk, which is a rich, piquant take on plain old whole milk. Old standby recipes that feature buttermilk include biscuits and pancakes, which are rockingly good. Or use it to make classic buttermilk salad dressing (page 24). Better yet, just pour it tall and drink its tangy, full-bodied fresh flavor. Note that the compound butters can be made with 4 ounces of store-bought butter if you've not made your own.

PREP AHEAD You'll need a clean, 1-pint jar with a snug-fitting lid. Before filling the jar with heavy cream, shake with water to make sure the jar doesn't leak.

1 cup heavy whipping cream
1/2 teaspoon kosher salt (optional)

INSTRUCTIONS Allow the cream to come to room temperature. Note that if you skip this step you can still make butter, but you will be doing the "shake the butter" dance for longer.

Pour the cream into a jar with a tight lid that's at least twice the capacity of the cream. Shake, shake, and shake the cream—butter will happen in 20 to 30 minutes. Shake vigorously, but be careful not to harm your wrists or hurl any high-speed glass jars across the room. The cream will thicken into stiff whipped cream first. Then, moments later, the butter will separate and form a solid mass apart from the buttermilk. Give a few more shakes to ensure you've finished the job.

Pour the buttermilk into a bowl and reserve. Continue to shake the butter by itself, pouring off the buttermilk, a couple more times.

Add just enough water to cover the solid butter, shake vigorously, and discard the liquid down the drain. Do this 3 or 4 more times, until the liquid from the jar is clear. (Note that if you plan to use the buttermilk, you don't want to mix it with this additional water.)

Spoon the butter into a bowl, pouring off any excess liquid. Add the salt, if desired. Or, if you're making compound butters, go ahead and add your other ingredients now. If you're using decorative molds, spoon the butter into them now. For a long stick of butter, pour it onto a 12-inch piece of waxed paper or parchment paper, and gently roll it up into a long and thin log. Whatever shape it takes, refrigerate for 30 to 45 minutes.

HOW TO STORE IT Refrigerate, tightly wrapped, up to 2 weeks. For long-term storage, double-wrap very tightly in plastic wrap, place in a sealable plastic bag, and freeze.

VARIATIONS To get the most out of your compound butter (see below), spoon it onto a 12-inch piece of waxed paper or parchment paper and gently roll it up, tightening it from the center outward as you go, into a long and thin log. Refrigerate to harden for about 45 minutes. Once firm, slice the butter in the paper into 1-inch pieces, and store in the freezer in a marked sealable plastic bag. You do not need to thaw butter before using; it can go straight from freezer to pan.

Walnut and Roasted Red Pepper Butter: Combine 9 walnut halves, toasted, 1/4 cup roasted red pepper (page 35), 1 teaspoon salt, and 1/2 cup room-temperature butter in a food processor. Process for 1 minute, until the pepper and the nuts are finely chopped and incorporated throughout. Enjoy over vegetables like roasted asparagus, spinach or potatoes.

Dill and Mustard Butter: Combine 2 tablespoons chopped fresh dill, 2 teaspoons prepared Mustard (see page 26), 1 teaspoon salt, and 1/2 cup room-temperature butter, and mash in a bowl. Melt over seared or grilled chicken or pork.

Caramelized Onion and Thyme Butter: Caramelize the onions by heating 2 tablespoons vegetable oil in a sauté pan over medium-high heat, adding 1 teaspoon salt. Add a chopped yellow onion, and when it starts to brown lower the heat to medium, stirring occasionally for 20 to 25 minutes until the onion turns golden brown all over. Let the onion cool, and combine with 1/2 cup room-temperature butter, 1 teaspoon salt, 2 tablespoons chopped fresh thyme, and 1/2 teaspoon black pepper in a food processor for 1 minute, until all the ingredients are finely minced and incorporated into the butter. This is wonderful with winter squash and makes a great pan sauce with steak.

yogurt cheese

Makes 2¹/₂ cups

TIME COMMITMENT
8 to 12 hours

Yogurt cheese—sometimes called strained yogurt, Greek yogurt, or *labneh*—is a sharper alternative to cream cheese, but it has a similar consistency and thus can easily take its place atop bagels or toast, stirred into mashed potatoes, or playing the starring role in cheesecake. Other attributes of this cheese include its utter simplicity to make, all the health benefits of yogurt, and a tangy personality. This staple item is in my kitchen at all times.

PREP AHEAD You'll need a clean, thin kitchen towel, either cotton or linen, thin enough to allow the moisture of the yogurt to pass through, but tightly woven enough not to allow all of the yogurt to pass through. Test-drive your towel with a tablespoon of yogurt to make sure it works. Butter muslin, available at kitchen supply stores, will also work, but avoid cheesecloth since it is too porous and the yogurt will just fall through. You'll also need a way to bind the corners of the cloth together into a small bag, and some kind of hook or string for hanging it over a sink or a large bowl.

1 (32-ounce) container plain yogurt

INSTRUCTIONS Line a large bowl with a clean, thin cotton or linen towel, positioning the middle of the towel in the bottom of the bowl. Pour the yogurt into its center. Gather together all 4 corners of the fabric and twist lightly; cloudy whey should be leaking out of the bottom. Tie the bundle up securely with a scarf, heavy string, or bungee cord. Hang the cord over a large bowl or over the sink—I usually tie it to the handle of the cabinet over the sink. Let it hang, undisturbed, overnight or for at least 8 hours.

You will find about 12 ounces of whey in the bowl, and very thick, spreadable tangy cheese in the towel. Drink the whey straight or in a smoothie or discard it. Scrape together the cheese and transfer to a small container with a tight lid.

HOW TO STORE IT Refrigerate, covered, up to 2 weeks.

VARIATIONS **Lemon Yogurt Cheese:** Add 1 teaspoon kosher salt and the juice of one-half lemon to the cheese.

Garlic Yogurt Cheese: Add 1 clove garlic, minced, and 2 tablespoons fresh chopped dill to the cheese.

Chive and Black Pepper Yogurt Cheese: Add 2 tablespoons fresh chives and several grinds of fresh black pepper to the cheese.

Cranberry and Green Onion Yogurt Cheese: Add ¹/₄ cup chopped dried cranberries and 1 minced green onion to the cheese.

queso blanco

Makes 1 (6- to 8-ounce)
cheese

TIME COMMITMENT
4 hours

Yes, you've got it, Spanish whiz that you are: white cheese. Mild, tender, and yielding, you know *queso blanco* as the filling of your chile relleno. It's quite similar to *paneer*, the Indian cheese, or the popular mass-produced Haloumi cheese. It tastes like the fresh milk from which it is made and has an amazing property: it does not melt or become gooey like most cheeses. Thus, this is a great cheese for grilling, frying, or otherwise torturing under high heat. My favorite way to enjoy *queso blanco* is sliced 1/8 inch thick and fried in 2 tablespoons olive oil for 3 minutes on each side, or until golden brown. Sprinkle with salt, squeeze on freshly squeezed lemon juice, and watch it disappear.

PREP AHEAD You'll need a cheese press for this recipe (see page 81) and 1 clean, thin kitchen towel or piece of butter muslin.

8 cups whole milk
1/4 cup apple cider vinegar
2 teaspoons kosher salt

INSTRUCTIONS Heat the milk over medium heat for 20 to 25 minutes, stirring occasionally to ensure that the temperature is the same throughout, until the temperature is 185° to 190°F. Slowly add the vinegar and stir gently, just until distributed evenly. Shut off the heat and allow the milk to sit, undisturbed, for about 10 minutes. You'll see curds separate from the whey and slightly pull away from the sides of the pot.

Once curds have formed, gently scoop them, using a slotted spoon, into a fine mesh sieve set over a bowl, and let them drain for a moment. Discard any whey that has dripped into the bottom of the bowl. Pour the curds into the bowl and toss with the salt. Move the curds into the center of a clean, thin kitchen towel. Tie up the towel, give it a gentle squeeze to help release additional moisture, and hang it over a bowl or over the sink for 30 to 45 minutes, until the dripping has stopped completely.

Transfer the drained cheese curds into a press and weight the cheese for 3 to 4 hours (see page 81). Once the cheese is firm, release it from the mold. It is now ready to eat.

HOW TO STORE IT Refrigerate, wrapped in waxed paper in the cheese section of your refrigerator, up to 1 week.

ricotta cheese

Makes 1¼ cups

TIME COMMITMENT
Less than 1 hour

This versatile, fresh cheese is an Italian staple and a crucial component of Meat, Cheese, and Spinach Filling (page 46). The process to make ricotta is simple, but be careful when handling the tiny, delicate curds, otherwise the end result will be crumbly and dry. Citric acid—also called sour salt—can be found at supermarkets or health foods stores. It's also available from online beer-making or candy-making supply retailers. A candy or frying thermometer is an absolute necessity for this and all other curd cheese–making recipes.

8 cups whole milk

1 teaspoon citric acid

¼ cup water

2 tablespoons half-and-half

1 teaspoon kosher salt

INSTRUCTIONS Pour the milk into a saucepan. In a small bowl, dissolve the citric acid in the water, then add it to the milk and set over medium heat. Stir to distribute the acid evenly. Clip your frying or candy thermometer to the side of the pot and make sure it does not touch the bottom.

When the temperature of the milk is 190°F (about 15 to 20 minutes), turn off the heat. Do not stir or disturb the milk, and let it sit for about 10 minutes to allow the curds to separate from the whey.

Gently strain the solids from the liquids in a fine mesh sieve. Don't press or squeeze them in any way. Once most of the liquid has dripped out, move the curds to a bowl and toss with the cream and salt.

HOW TO STORE IT Refrigerate, covered, up to 1 week.

MAKING YOUR OWN CHEESE PRESS

If you want to transform fluid cheese curds into a firm cheese, they must be pressed together under a bit of pressure and weight. The tool for this job is a cheese press, and you can order one from New England Cheesemaking Supply Company (www.cheese making.com). But why spend money and storage space on an item that you won't use every day? Instead, I recommend making your own. First, wash and dry an empty 28-ounce can. Make sure it is entirely clean and devoid of all odors. Use a can opener to remove both the top and the bottom of the can.

Lay a clean kitchen towel over a flat board, and position the can on top of the bottom lid. Pour the cheese curds into the can and gently (and carefully) press them down with your fingers to create a flat surface. Lay the top of the can on top of the curds. Cover with a heavy weight. I use a large squat and stable jar filled with water.

To release the cheese after pressing, remove the weight. Push down on the top of the can and lift the can up, leaving a sandwich of cheese between the top and bottom of the can. Then gently remove the top. Cover with a small plate, invert, and gently remove the bottom.

ricotta salata

Makes 1 (6 to 8-ounce)
cheese

TIME COMMITMENT
6 to 8 days

This sliceable cheese has a texture and saltiness similar to that of Romano cheese, though it's not nearly as complex. It can be eaten on its own, but it's also a great cooking cheese, tossed with pasta or crumbled onto soups or salads. This cheese is not one that will get better with age, so it's best eaten within a week.

PREP AHEAD You'll need a cheese press for this recipe (see page 81) and several thin kitchen towels, cloth napkins, or pieces of cheesecloth for the curing process.

> 1 1/4 cups fresh Ricotta Cheese curds (page 80)
> 4 teaspoons kosher salt, or more if needed

INSTRUCTIONS Pour the cheese curds into a cheese press and press at room temperature for 3 to 4 hours, until solid. Once the cheese has come together, gently coat the exterior with 2 teaspoons of the salt (or more), then wrap it in a clean kitchen towel. Place the wrapped cheese on a plate, and refrigerate for 2 days.

Remove the cheese from the fridge, rub with 1 more teaspoon salt, and replace the "bandage" with a clean cloth. Let it sit for another 2 days. Repeat once more; the cheese should be quite firm.

Once it's ready to eat, brush off as much of the salt as possible, and slice from the center out—as you would a pie. Enjoy immediately.

HOW TO STORE IT Refrigerate, wrapped in waxed paper, in the cheese section, up to 1 week.

VARIATION If you're planning to offer this cheese as a gift, you can decorate it with a flattened sprig of fresh herbs or colorful edible flowers. Simply lay the decoration on the bottom of the press before spooning your curds into the mold.

8 | jam it

PRESERVES, CURDS, AND FRUIT BUTTER

Making jams and preserves, the quintessential kitchen craft, is the easiest way to add your own handiwork to the food pantry for a fraction of the price.

When making my own jams, I prefer not to add pectin. There's nothing wrong with it, but if you stick to fruits that have a good amount of natural pectin, or supplement low-pectin fruits with sugar and fresh lemon and its seeds—crucial components for thickening and preserving—then adding extra pectin isn't necessary. Buying it in powder or liquid form seems unnecessary when it's just as easy to call on the natural pectin available in real fruit.

A few words about the recipes in this chapter: Don't use a sugar substitute, or reduce the amount of sugar or lemon juice—though you can make it sweeter if that's to your taste. Buy top-quality fruit that is ripe, sweet, unbruised, and good enough to eat by itself. Inferior fruit will yield inferior results.

Get creative, and get fruity. It's time to jam on jam.

strawberry jam

Makes about 10 (8-ounce)
or 20 (4-ounce) jars

TIME COMMITMENT
2 to 3 days

Unlike the cooperative apple, the accommodating cranberry, or the boil-it-and-it's-done plum, the strawberry is a low-pectin fruit, which means that it and all other berries need a little boost to thicken up. In this case, the strawberries get help from the lemon and its seeds. This take on one of the most beloved of all jams is easy to make, but it's a slow jam. I've found that the extra time is worth it to produce a flavorful finished product with a stunning jewel-like color and an even distribution of berries.

PREP AHEAD A mammoth stockpot is required for this recipe as the fruit will create a tremendous amount of foam—about 4 times the volume of the fruit itself. Trust me, there is nothing worse than scrubbing sticky berry mess out from under the burner. You'll need 10 half-pint jars, or their equivalent, for this cooking project. Make sure they are free of rust and odors and the lids seal tightly. If you are planning on giving these as gifts, make sure you indicate in some manner the contents and date prepared.

6 pints fresh, perfect, sweet strawberries

9 cups sugar

3/4 cup freshly squeezed lemon juice (from about 5 lemons), rinds (kept whole) and seeds reserved

INSTRUCTIONS Wash, dry, stem, and slice (or chop) the berries. In a large bowl, toss them gently with the sugar and lemon juice; don't bruise your fruit. Let them macerate for 4 to 8 hours to release their juice. Tie up the lemon seeds in cheesecloth or an empty tea bag.

Transfer the strawberries and the lemon rinds and seeds to a very large stockpot. Bring to a boil over medium-high heat and boil for 3 minutes, then turn the heat to medium and simmer for 10 to 15 minutes, stirring occasionally.

Skim off the loads and loads of foam that will surface—this is best done with a large metal spoon. Remove as much of the foam as possible, as this will give your jam a clear, brilliant color. Allow the jam to cool in the pot, then transfer to a wide-mouthed bowl or baking dish. Discard the lemon rinds and seeds. Let the jam sit, uncovered, stirring occasionally, overnight. This will help the jam thicken and keep the fruit from separating from the syrup. If the jam is not to your desired thickness, allow it to sit for 1 more day.

Transfer the jam to jars, ensuring that the lip and threads of the jars remain clean and unsticky.

HOW TO STORE IT Refrigerate up to 4 months.

HOW TO CAN IT Carefully read through the canning directions on page 88 before you begin. Macerate and then cook the jam as directed, but continue to simmer rapidly, stirring often, until it reaches the jell point, checked with a thermometer—you want it to register 221°F—or the ice-cold plate test (see page 89). This should take about 30 minutes. Ladle into sterilized half-pint jars, leaving 1/4 inch headspace, and process in a hot-water bath for 10 minutes.

NOTES ON HOW TO CAN PRESERVES AND PICKLES

We youngsters think of a can as something that wraps around SpaghettiOs, or as the container that goes into the recycle bin after we've dumped our organic, microwavable split pea soup into a bowl. But in the olden days, long before factory modernization was king, canning—yes, we know, it's actually done with jars, so why not call it jarring?—was a home process that put the season's bounty onto cupboard shelves for leaner times. Nowadays, home cooks are often put off by canning, mistakenly thinking it's a mysterious process of old wives' know-how, hot, sticky wax, and messy pots that can explode on a dime. But in truth, if you can boil water, you can put up preserves and pickles. You just need to make sure that the vinegar you use for your pickles has an acidity level of at least 5 percent, and that all of your equipment is squeaky-clean.

If you decide you want to can your own chicken soup or tuna, in other words—foods that are not preserved with hefty measures of sugar, salt, or vinegar—you are going to have to buy a pressure canner and learn how to use it. Since my kitchen barely has room to store a cake pan that's not in use, I don't have a pressure canner, and the recipes in this book don't require one.

Basically, all you need to do to can is fill a jar with food, top it with a lid, and "process" it, which simply means boil the jar in water for a short amount of time. Here's the nitty-gritty on how to handle the recipes in this book, from the equipment to putting your filled jars in the cupboard.

Ready the equipment. You can use the same cooking pot, wooden spoon for stirring, and metal spoon for skimming that you use for making your refrigerated preserves and pickles. You just need to make sure the pot is heavy and nonreactive—in other words, no aluminum, unlined copper, or cast iron. A thermometer—a combination candy and deep-frying model—is handy for knowing when your preserves have thickened sufficiently to ladle into jars. Or you can go the low-tech route and have a few small saucers in the freezer for testing the jell point (below). You'll need Mason canning jars, which are widemouthed for easy filling, and two-piece caps, a self-sealing lid held in place by a metal ring band. Once you have the jars, you can reuse them, as long as you haven't chipped or cracked them along the threads or rim. If the ring bands aren't rusted or bent, they can be reused, too. But the lids have no second life. That skinny, gummy gasket that seals them on the jar rim works one time only. Consider investing in a good ladle and a widemouthed funnel, too, so everything goes into the jar, rather than on the countertop, and have a narrow plastic spatula, chopstick, or plastic knife on hand for alleviating air bubbles (see Fill the Jars), a clean kitchen towel or two for cleaning up the jar rims, and tongs for retrieving the lids from their sterilizing water.

Once the jars are full and capped, you need to process them in a hot-water bath. That means you either have to buy a water-bath canner, which is basically a big pot with a lid and a sturdy metal rack that raises the jars off the pot bottom, or you have to rig one up, using a wide, deep pot and a metal rack that are already in your cupboard. Fortunately, this setup is also good for sterilizing the jars before you fill them. Finally, you'll want jar tongs or tongs for lifting the jars out of their hot baths—both the one for sterilizing and the one for processing—and a metal rack or folded kitchen towel where the jars can rest as they cool down.

Sterilize the jars and lids. It's best to time the sterilizing of the jars and lids so they are still piping hot when you are ready to fill them, so check the recipe you are making to figure out when to start the water boiling. First, wash the jars in hot, soapy water. Then stand the jars upright on a metal rack in a large pot (here's where you press that water-bath canner into service) on the stove top, add hot water to cover by at least an inch, bring to

a boil, and boil for 10 minutes at altitudes of less than 1,000 feet, adding 1 minute for each additional 1,000 feet. Turn off the heat and leave the jars in the hot water until you are ready to fill them, or drain them and move them to a warm oven to keep them hot. While the jars are bubbling away, put the lids in a saucepan, add water to cover, bring to a simmer (boiling will ruin their seal), and remove from the heat. Leave them covered in their hot water as well. If you have an up-to-date dishwasher with a sterilize cycle, you can skip boiling the jars and instead run them through the cycle, then leave them on the "heated dry" setting until you are ready to fill them.

Test the jell point. You can test if your preserves are ready for putting into jars, that is, have reached the jell point, by clipping the thermometer onto the pot when the mixture starts boiling and then waiting until it registers the correct temperature (see individual recipes for the temperature you want), or you can use the ice-cold plate method: When the mixture has cooked the amount of time indicated and looks nice and thick, drop a big spoonful of it on an ice-cold plate, let it sit in the freezer for 2 minutes, and then check to see if it holds its shape by lightly pushing it with a fingertip. If it wrinkles slightly or appears to be properly thickened, it's

//CONTINUED

ready. If it doesn't, continue boiling for a few minutes and check again.

Fill the jars. Once your preserves or pickles are ready to decant, remove a jar from the hot water (or dishwasher or oven), drain it, and fill with the food, using the funnel and ladle to prevent spills and filling just short of the rim, as directed in each recipe. This gap is known as headspace, and it allows for the expansion that naturally occurs when the filled jars are processed in the water bath. If there's no gap, whatever you are processing might break the seal and leak out. Next, if you are making thick preserves, stick a slim plastic spatula, chopstick, or plastic knife into the jar and raise it and lower it a few times to force out any trapped air bubbles. When dealing with pickles, the thin liquid usually spreads evenly. But with thicker foods, you need to be diligent on this Bubble Patrol, because bacteria can grow in empty spaces. This is also the reason you need to fill the jar nearly to the top. Too much headspace and bacteria can sneak in and spoil all your work.

Dampen a kitchen towel and wipe the rim of the jar clean. Any residue can cause a seal to fail. Then, using tongs, fish a lid out of the hot water, place it, gasket side down, on the rim, and screw on the ring band. Repeat until all of the jars are filled. Don't

dump the water in the pot. You can use it for the water bath.

Process in a water bath. Place the jars on the rack in the pot, making sure they are not touching one another. Add boiling water as needed to cover the jars by about 1 to 2 inches. Cover the pot, bring the water to a full boil, and boil for the time indicated in the recipe, usually 10 to 15 minutes, depending on what's being processed and, in the case of the green beans and ketchup, the altitude. Turn off the heat, uncover, and, using the jar tongs, lift the jars from the pot. Place them upright on the rack or folded towel, spacing them at least 1 inch apart so air can circulate, and let cool naturally.

As the jars cool down, you may hear the lids ping, a reassuring signal that the vacuum seal has taken. When the jars have cooled completely, check the seal on each lid. The center should be slightly depressed. Press on the center of the lid with a fingertip. If it stays down, the seal is good. If it pops up, the seal didn't take, and you need to store preserves or pickles in the refrigerator for no longer than the time specified in the recipe.

Store the bounty. Sure, you're pickle proud and jam joyous and you want to show off the fruits of your labor. But here's the rub: your expertly sealed jars need sensory deprivation—somewhere cool and dark—because light can alter the color and flavor of what's inside. So slip the jars into a cool, dark, dry cupboard, where they will keep happily for up to 1 year.

Before opening a jar of canned food, always inspect it: if the seal is broken or its contents have mold or emit a foul odor, discard immediately. To take extra precaution against the unlikely but possible growth of any harmful bacteria while in storage, boil the contents of every jar for 10 minutes before eating.

orange marmalade

Makes 10 (8-ounce) or
20 (4-ounce) jars

TIME COMMITMENT
2 days

Sweet but tart, this marmalade has a lot going for it: tender fruit, piquant flavor, and vibrant color. While it is possible to use sweet oranges, like navels, the finished product would lack the complexity of one made from tart fruit. Be sure to avoid using thin-skinned fruits, like Satsumas or Mandarins, as the results will be too watery. This orange marmalade functions as more than just a toast topper. Rub it on a roast chicken, add a lump of it to make a salad dressing tangy, or spread it between layers of cake.

PREP AHEAD Marmalade should be cooked in a large stockpot to help contain some of the foamy overflow. You will need 10 half-pint jars, or their equivalent, to store your bounty. Make sure they are free of rust and odors and the lids seal tightly. Prepare a label that lists the contents and date prepared.

5 pounds tart oranges, like Seville or Valencia
4 lemons
7 to 8 cups sugar

INSTRUCTIONS Scrub the skins of the oranges and lemons well, and dry them. Peel the skins from the fruit, and set the fruit aside—keep it covered and airtight. Mince the skins and pith; or, if you have food processor technology, now is the time to use it. You can achieve the right size and thinness by running the skins through the thin slicing blade twice. Cover the skins with water in a large bowl and let them soak overnight.

The next day, chop the orange and lemon pulp into small bits, reserving as much of the juice as you can as you go and saving the seeds. Tie the seeds up in cheesecloth or an empty tea bag.

Drain the water from the skins and transfer them to a large stockpot. Add the fruit pulp, juice, and seed bag. Bring to a boil, then let it simmer gently over medium to medium-low heat for about 2 hours, stirring occasionally and scraping up from the bottom to prevent sticking.

Add the sugar—starting with 7 cups, then adding up to 1 cup more, depending on the sweetness of the fruit—and thoroughly combine it with the fruit. Let it simmer about 30 minutes longer, or until the marmalade is sweet and thick.

Transfer the marmalade to jars, wipe the rim clean, and cover.

HOW TO STORE IT You can refrigerate the marmalade up to 4 months.

HOW TO CAN IT Carefully read through the canning directions on page 88 before you begin. Soak the orange and lemon peels and cook them with the pulp and sugar as directed until sweet and thick, then test for the jell point, checked with a thermometer—you want it to register 221°F—or the ice-cold plate test. Ladle into sterilized half-pint jars, leaving 1/4 inch headspace, and process in a hot-water bath for 15 minutes.

apple butter

Makes 3 1/2 to 4 cups

TIME COMMITMENT
3 hours

The creamy consistency of fruit butters is remarkable given that they contain no dairy or fat. Choose any variety of sweet apples you like for this recipe—Pink Lady, Red Delicious, Fuji, and such—but use a combination of three varieties for a more complex flavor. Avoid tart apples like Granny Smiths. While most apple butter recipes call for boiling or steaming the apples, I much prefer to roast them, which gives a luscious caramel color and intense flavor. Because of its smoothness and beautiful, rich color, apple butter makes a great gift. Pack it into artful jars and decorate them with your signature style (a fancy doily? a pretty sticker label? a simple monogrammed note?). If you'd rather keep all the apple butter to yourself, consider making apple fruit leather with some of it (page 103).

PREP AHEAD You will need clean jars to store your bounty. Make sure they are free of rust and odors and the lids seal tightly. Prepare a label that lists the contents and date prepared.

8 pounds sweet apples

2 tablespoons freshly squeezed lemon juice

1/3 cup golden brown sugar

1 teaspoon kosher salt

2 teaspoons ground cinnamon

1/2 teaspoon ground allspice

1/4 teaspoon ground cardamom

INSTRUCTIONS Preheat the oven to 350°F.

Peel, quarter, and core the apples. Lightly oil 2 large rimmed baking sheets. Arrange the apple pieces in a single layer and bake them for 2 hours, or until brown and fragrant. After 1 hour, swap the positions of the 2 baking sheets and rotate each sheet 180 degrees, so the front apples are now at the back of the oven and vice versa.

In a food processor or blender, puree the fruit for about 4 minutes, or until very smooth, scraping down the sides of the bowl as necessary. Add the lemon juice, sugar, salt, cinnamon, allspice, and cardamom, and puree again for 2 to 3 minutes more, until all the spices are incorporated and the texture is nearly puddinglike.

HOW TO STORE IT Refrigerate, in a covered glass jar, up to 1 month.

lemon curd

Makes about 2 cups

TIME COMMITMENT
1 hour

I am a devoted fan of this English delicacy. Slather this very smooth, very lemony curd on crepes and toast, or layer a yellow cake with it for outstanding results, particularly when paired with fresh strawberries. Of course, my preferred vehicle for enjoying lemon curd is a spoon.

PREP AHEAD You will need clean jars to store your bounty. Make sure they are free of rust and odors and the lids seal tightly. Prepare a label that lists the contents and date prepared.

- 6 eggs plus 1 egg yolk
- 1 cup sugar
- 1 1/2 cups freshly squeezed lemon juice (from about 12 lemons)
- 10 tablespoons butter, cut into small pieces
- Zest of 2 lemons, removed in large pieces with a vegetable peeler

INSTRUCTIONS In a large saucepan, with a whisk, beat the eggs and egg yolk thoroughly, then whisk in the sugar and lemon juice. Stir together until thoroughly combined. The sugar should be completely integrated into the liquids, which will result in a much creamier curd.

Place the pot over medium heat and gently warm the mixture. After 3 minutes, add the butter and the zest pieces. Whisk constantly for 7 to 8 minutes, until the butter melts and the mixture becomes very thick.

Pour the curd into a clean glass jar and let it cool at room temperature, uncovered. Remove the zest and discard. Eat warm, or cover and refrigerate for about an hour.

HOW TO STORE IT Refrigerate, in a covered glass jar, up to 10 days.

9 | sugar it

SWEET TREATS

The recipes in this chapter are a collection of some of my favorite junk foods deconstructed and demystified. It's one thing to eat butter and sugar—neither a health food by any stretch. But it's quite another to chow down on artificial color and high fructose corn syrup for no good reason. If you're going to enjoy the fruity indulgence of a flaky toaster tart, let it be one with a wholesome, toothsome crust. You are worthy of marshmallows that are tender and fluffy. Your conscience deserves a chocolate sandwich cookie with crisp wafers and a restrained, mature sweetness. And fruit leather—real fruit leather—needs nothing more than just the fruit to be intensely concentrated and flavorful.

These sweet treats make perfect gifts. Present them in a well-decorated box with a personalized label, or throw them into a classic cellophane bag. Or simply show up at your next brunch, tea, or picnic with an assortment of your best efforts. You'll be treated like a rock star by whoever is the lucky recipient of your homemade sweet handicrafts.

toaster tarts

Makes 10 to 12 tarts

TIME COMMITMENT
About 2 hours

You will be brunch royalty if you bring a fresh batch of these childhood favorites. Unlike the ones sold in foil two-packs, these have all the wholesome cred of homemade pie. Fill the tarts with homemade strawberry jam (page 86), apple butter (page 93), or lemon curd (page 95). If you don't have any handy, buy some of the good stuff. This is the time to splurge. Homemade butter, as wonderful as it is, is not a good choice for this recipe because its moisture content is too unreliable to produce a perfect crust. Homemade lard (page 67), however, would be ideal here.

CRUST

1/2 cup unsalted butter (not homemade)

1/2 cup shortening or Lard (page 67)

3 cups all-purpose flour

2 tablespoons sugar

1 1/2 teaspoons kosher salt

1 1/2 teaspoons cider vinegar

5 tablespoons ice-cold water, or more as needed

ICING

1 cup confectioners' sugar

2 tablespoons water

TARTS

1 egg

5 tablespoons jam, Apple Butter (page 93), or Lemon Curd (page 95), or more as needed

INSTRUCTIONS To make the crust, chop the butter and shortening into 1/2-inch cubes, and chill in the freezer for about 15 minutes while you assemble the rest of the ingredients.

Mix the flour, sugar, and salt in a food processor, if you have one. If you don't, mix by hand in a chilled bowl. Add the cold butter and shortening, and pulse until combined. If working by hand, quickly coat the butter and shortening with the dry ingredients and, working with 2 knives, cut the butter and shortening into the flour until it forms coarse crumbs. Add the vinegar and water and combine. If needed, keep adding water, 1 teaspoon at a time, just until the dough holds together. (The key here is to use as little liquid as possible.)

Bring the dough together on a floured work surface, cut it in half, shape each piece into a flat rectangle about 1/2 inch thick, wrap each rectangle in plastic wrap, and refrigerate for 1 hour.

To make the icing, while the dough chills, stir together the confectioners' sugar and water.

To assemble the tarts, preheat the oven to 350°F and beat the egg in a small bowl. Have a pastry brush near.

Remove the first dough rectangle from the refrigerator, unwrap, and roll it out on a floured work surface using a floured rolling pin, keeping it in the best rectangle shape you can muster, about $1/8$ inch thick. If the dough gets too soft to work with, chill for 20 minutes in the fridge or 5 minutes in the freezer.

Measure twice, cut once. Grab a tape measure, and nick the edges of the crust to allow for as many 3 by 4-inch rectangles as possible. When you have the sizing right, cut out your rectangles with a pizza cutter, knife, or scraper. From 1 dough rectangle, you will likely have 10 to 12 pieces, enough for 5 to 6 tarts. Brush each piece of dough with beaten egg.

Eyeball 2 similarly sized pieces. Spoon 1 scant teaspoon of jam into the center of 1 of the pieces of dough and smooth it over, leaving a $1/2$-inch margin on all sides. Cover with its twin piece of dough, egg wash side down, and gently flatten the 2 pieces together, squeezing out as much air as possible and being careful not to let the filling leak out the sides.

With a dinner fork, press the edges of the tart together, and gently poke 3 or 4 sets of holes into the top of the tart. Brush with the icing. Don't worry too much if the icing doesn't go on evenly, as it will become transparent as it bakes. Using your scraper or a spatula, carefully transfer the tart to an ungreased baking sheet.

Assemble the remaining tarts. Bake for about 20 to 25 minutes, or just until light brown. The theory here is that you'll finish baking them later in the toaster oven when you're ready to eat them. If you want to eat them all right away, bake for 10 minutes more, or until golden brown all over.

Repeat the above with the second dough rectangle.

HOW TO STORE IT Cooled, prebaked tarts can be kept in a sealable plastic bag in the freezer for 3 months. Toast in a toaster or toaster oven when ready to eat.

marshmallows

Makes about 36 medium (1¹/4-inch) or 16 large (2-inch) marshmallows

TIME COMMITMENT
2 hours

These light, fluffy, and flavorful clouds kick the butt off anything jet-puffed by a wide country mile. They will stand up to stick and flame on your next campout and are dreamy when paired with a slab of chocolate and homemade graham crackers (page 107). They're even worth firing up the Weber on the patio just to marvel at their rich, toasty flavor. If you're fire-toasting, make large (2-inch) marshmallows.

²/3 cup water, divided

3 (¹/4-ounce) envelopes unflavored gelatin

1 cup granulated sugar

1 cup light corn syrup

Pinch of kosher salt

1 teaspoon vanilla extract

1 cup confectioners' sugar, for dusting

INSTRUCTIONS Lightly oil the inside of an 8 by 8-inch pan with vegetable oil. Generously coat with confectioners' sugar; set aside.

Pour ¹/3 cup of the water into the bowl of a stand mixer. Sprinkle the gelatin over the water, and let stand for about 10 minutes, or until the gelatin has softened.

In a saucepan, off heat, combine the remaining ¹/3 cup water and the granulated sugar, corn syrup, and salt. Place the pan over medium-high heat. Clip a candy thermometer to the inside of the pan and make sure it does not touch the bottom. Cook the mixture without stirring until it reaches 240°F. Brush down the sides of the pan with a pastry brush (or a clean paintbrush reserved for kitchen use only), dipped in water, to gently wipe away any residual sugar crystals.

// CONTINUED

marshmallows, CONTINUED

With the mixer on low speed, very carefully add the hot syrup to the softened gelatin. Add the vanilla, increase the speed to medium-high, and beat for 8 to 13 minutes, until the mixture becomes very white, stiff, and sticky.

Spread the mixture into the prepared pan using a lightly oiled spatula. With wet hands, press the batter evenly into the corners of the pan. Set aside for at least 1 hour, or until the mixture is firm and cool.

Sift the confectioners' sugar into a shallow dish or bowl. Run a wet knife around the edge of the cooled pan to loosen the marshmallow sheet. Remove the marshmallows from the pan. Cut into 16 or 36 squares, wetting the knife often to keep it from sticking. Toss each marshmallow in the confectioners' sugar until completely coated.

HOW TO STORE IT Store marshmallows in a single layer or in layers separated by waxed paper. They will keep for at least 1 month when stored airtight at moderate temperature.

VARIATIONS Substitute sifted unsweetened cocoa or toasted shredded coconut for the confectioners' sugar used to coat the marshmallows, or fold 1 cup finely chopped cacao nibs, toasted almonds, mini chocolate chips, dried cranberries—or any combination thereof—into the stiff marshmallow mixture before spreading.

apple fruit leather

Makes 12 to 16 (1-inch)
strips of leather

TIME COMMITMENT
6 to 8 hours

Take stunning fresh fruit, puree it until smooth, spread it flat, and remove its moisture. What remains is portable, intensely sweet and tangy, and preserved, naturally, for several weeks. Homemade fruit leather is the predecessor for various popular gummy fruit snacks marketed to kids, but this, the real deal, has a mature sophistication that doesn't come in shades of bright blue. Apple is the most basic of fruit leathers, as the fruit is widely available and quite sweet, and it has a good amount of pectin to help it dry and solidify. Feel free, however, to experiment with other high-pectin fruits, like cranberries or plums. If you don't have the time to make Apple Butter (page 93), substitute applesauce. But look for one made only with high-quality fruit.

3 cups Apple Butter (page 93) or applesauce

INSTRUCTIONS Preheat the oven to 150°F. Or, if your oven can't get below 170°F, set it to its lowest temperature and lodge a wooden spoon into the door to keep it ajar.

Line a large rimmed baking sheet with parchment paper and spread the apple butter into a large rectangle of even thickness, about 1/8 to 1/4 inch.

Place the pan in the center of the oven for 5 to 7 hours, checking after 5 hours. The fruit should be sticky but not wet, throughout; the center is usually the last to dry.

Once sticky all over, remove the pan from the oven and gently peel the fruit from the parchment paper, releasing it from all 4 edges first, then peeling up the middle. Flip it over, and return it to the oven for another 30 minutes.

Tear off a clean piece of parchment or waxed paper larger than the sheet of fruit leather. Roll 2 inches of the paper over the fruit, then from the long side roll the whole thing up like a jelly roll. With a sharp knife, slice the rolled-up log into 1-inch pieces.

HOW TO STORE IT You can store, refrigerated, for at least 4 months.

VARIATIONS Substitute 1 1/2 cups of pureed bananas or pureed strawberries for 1 1/2 cups of the apple butter.

chocolate sandwich cookies

Makes about 24 cookies

TIME COMMITMENT
2 hours

In my humble opinion, this is the perfect sandwich cookie: deep in chocolate, crisp, and rich, and the perfect foil for the sweetness of the white filling. True, they don't come wrapped neatly in a pretty package, but they dunk into milk as well as anything found on the shelf, and their flavor and texture far surpass anything from a factory's cookie cutter. These cookies look particularly pretty when decorated with a stamp. You can use any stamp so long as it is reserved for cooking purposes only, is completely clean, and is free of ink.

COOKIES

1 cup granulated sugar or superfine sugar

2 1/2 cups all-purpose flour

1/2 cup unsweetened Dutch-process cocoa powder

2 teaspoons baking powder

1/2 teaspoon kosher salt

3/4 cup (1 1/2 sticks) unsalted butter, chopped into cubes

2 egg yolks

2 teaspoons vanilla extract

1/2 cup bittersweet or semisweet chocolate chips or chunks, melted and cooled

2 tablespoons water

FILLING

1 cup confectioners' sugar

1 tablespoon corn syrup

1 1/2 tablespoons evaporated milk

INSTRUCTIONS To make the cookies in a food processor, start by processing the granulated sugar for 30 seconds, then adding the flour, baking powder, salt, and cocoa to combine. If not using a food processor, in a bowl, combine the superfine sugar with the flour, cocoa powder, baking powder, and salt. Add the butter and combine just until

coarse crumbs form. Blend in the egg yolks and vanilla. Scrape the melted chocolate into the batter and mix to combine completely. Add the water, 1 tablespoon at a time, until the dough comes together when squeezed in your hand. Note that the batter will be crumbly, but cohesive.

Preheat the oven to 400°F, and grease 2 baking sheets. Adjust the oven rack to the center of the oven.

Gather the dough together on top of a piece of parchment paper or wax paper with a scraper nearby. Divide the dough in half, and shape each piece into a flat square. Set one square aside, and roll out the first square by covering it with a second sheet of parchment or wax paper, and flattening it into a large rectangle about 13 by 15 inches (the dough will be about 1/4 inch thick).

Cut out as many cookies as you can using an inverted glass or a cookie cutter, each about 3 inches in diameter or to your preference. Note that a pushing and twisting motion will yield a cleaner break in the dough. Gather the remaining scraps of dough and cut out more cookies; you should be able to comfortably fit a dozen on each baking sheet. Note that a scraper is a great tool for moving the cookies from counter to baking sheet. If you're using decorative stamps, use them now.

Bake the first sheet by itself for 7 to 9 minutes, or until the edges are slightly dark, they smell very chocolaty, and the cookies are brown on the bottom. The cookies will rise during baking, but flatten out again once cool. Let them cool on the baking sheet for 2 minutes before transferring to a wire rack.

Meanwhile, repeat the rolling and the cutting with the second half of the dough. Roll out the scrap pieces of dough between the papers again, and cut out as many cookies as possible. If the dough gets too soft to work with, leave on parchment and chill for 20 minutes in the fridge or 5 minutes in the freezer.

Bake the cookies as above. Cool all the cookies on a rack for about 30 minutes, or until they are cooled to room temperature, before sandwiching.

To make the filling, in a large bowl combine the confectioners' sugar, corn syrup, and milk until they form a sticky mass. Spoon the mixture into a pastry bag. Alternatively, use a sealable plastic bag, coaxing all of the filling into 1 corner and snipping off just a tiny corner of the bag with scissors.

To assemble the cookies, with the flat side of a cookie facing up, squeeze out 1 to 2 teaspoons of icing onto the center of a cookie and lay the flat side of another cookie on top, giving it a twist to spread the icing around. In a perfect world, you've used enough icing to just reach the edge of the cookie, but not so much that it's leaking out the sides. Note that as the cookies sit, the icing will spread a bit more. It's best to let the cookies firm up a little before serving, about 1 hour.

HOW TO STORE IT Store at room temperature, in an airtight container, up to 1 week.

graham crackers

Makes about 3 dozen
3-inch square crackers

TIME COMMITMENT
About 1 hour

The key to making perfect graham crackers is rolling the dough evenly. Homemade crackers often look rustic, but if you're a perfectionist, have a ruler handy to ensure that each cracker is exactly the same size, or break out the cookie cutters and decorative stamps to give them fresh-from-the-factory polish. Together with homemade marshmallows (page 101), these crackers make a mean S'more. Try them also as sandwich cookies by layering cream cheese or Yogurt Cheese (page 78) between crackers.

1 1/2 cups whole wheat flour

1 cup all-purpose flour

1 teaspoon kosher salt

2 teaspoons baking powder

1/3 cup chilled unsalted butter, cut into small pieces

1/4 cup honey

1/4 cup blackstrap molasses

1/3 cup plus 4 tablespoons sugar

1/4 cup whole milk

1/2 teaspoon vanilla extract

INSTRUCTIONS In a bowl or a food processor, mix or pulse the whole wheat flour, all-purpose flour, salt, and baking powder. Cut in the butter or, if using a food processor, add the butter and pulse until the dough is the consistency of coarse crumbs. Add the honey, molasses, and the 1/3 cup sugar and combine. Then add the milk and vanilla, bringing it all together into a stiff dough.

Lightly oil 2 baking sheets. On a work surface, cut the dough in half. Shape the first half into a rectangle and place in the center of a sheet of parchment paper. Lay another sheet of parchment paper over the dough. Roll, trying to keep the dough as rectangular as possible.

The dough should be 1/4 inch thick, and about 12 by 15 inches. Lightly prick the dough all over with the tines of a fork. Sprinkle evenly with 2 tablespoons of the sugar, and roll the sugar gently into the top of the dough with a floured pin. Using a knife or a fluted pastry cutter (for the cute wavy edges in the picture opposite), trim the edges of the dough rectangle to yield neat crackers (or leave them uneven if you prefer). Cut into approximately 3-inch squares. Using a spatula, carefully transfer the crackers to the prepared baking sheets, leaving a little space between them. Repeat the process with the second half of the dough. Freeze the crackers for 15 minutes.

Meanwhile, preheat the oven to 350°F.

Bake the chilled dough for 18 to 22 minutes, until just a little browned at the edges. Cool completely and enjoy.

HOW TO STORE IT Store in an airtight container, up to 2 weeks. You can also freeze the crackers for 2 months, allowing 2 hours to thaw before eating.

VARIATION Add 2 teaspoons cinnamon to the 4 tablespoons sugar, and sprinkle evenly over the dough before cutting the crackers.

10 | freeze it

FROZEN CONFECTIONS

If your kitchen is as small as mine, you probably don't have storage space for a cabinet hog such as an ice cream maker. Those in pursuit of frozen fun, however, have other options. You can always fill an ice cube tray with any of the recipes below, cover it with plastic wrap, and insert toothpicks for sticks. But if you're ready to make an investment in frozen assets, treat yourself to a set of novelty frozen pop molds. I'm in love with the Tovolo line of molds for a number of reasons: they freeze into eye-catching retro shapes; they can be unmolded one at a time; and they have a built-in drip tray at the base of the stick to prevent splatter on your shirt. Sheer genius.

Here's a simple bit of science to remember when making frozen pops: stuff expands slightly when it freezes; thus, remember to leave $1/4$ inch at the top of the mold, so that your pops have room to grow. And there's nothing worse than having the excitement of diving into your frozen confection quashed by a half-melted pop that won't release and a sad, empty stick in your hand. Here's what I've found to be the most reliable way to get your pops out of the molds intact: Holding the stick, submerge the mold in a tall drinking glass of hot tap water for 20 to 30 seconds. The outside of the pop should feel room temperature when it's ready to be released, and it will release easily. Never yank hard on the stick.

mango and lime pops

Makes 6 (4-ounce) pops

TIME COMMITMENT
7 hours

Muy refrescante, muy tropical. The bright sweetness of mangoes, when you can find them in good shape, is enhanced by the tang of the citrus. The combination will blow a Caribbean breeze your way when the weather is scorching. And speaking of scorching . . . adjust the cayenne pepper to your own tolerance for heat. I like mine *muy caliente.*

1/2 cup sugar

1/2 cup water

2 small ripe mangoes, peeled, pitted, and cut into chunks

1/2 cup lime juice (from about 4 limes)

1/2 to 1 teaspoon cayenne pepper

Pinch of kosher salt

INSTRUCTIONS Make a simple syrup by combining the sugar and water in a small saucepan and warming over medium heat just until the sugar dissolves. Cool completely.

Combine the syrup, mangoes, lime juice, cayenne pepper, and salt in a blender or food processor. Blend well, pour into molds, and freeze for at least 6 hours or overnight.

HOW TO STORE IT Freeze up to 3 months. Store in the molds or release, wrap well in waxed paper, and store in a marked sealable plastic bag.

Opposite: Mango and Lime Pops and Watermelon Pops (page 112)

watermelon pops

Makes 6 (4-ounce) pops

TIME COMMITMENT
7 hours

The flavor of the melon is certainly the star here, but that little kick of mint and citrus gives it a further gentle nudge into the spotlight. Of course, starting with seedless watermelon will facilitate the process, but picking out the seeds before blending is not too laborious a task. Oils and extracts are not always interchangeable, but in this recipe either will suffice.

5 cups chopped fresh watermelon, seeds removed

1 teaspoon mint-infused oil or extract

1 teaspoon orange-infused oil or extract

$1/2$ teaspoon kosher salt

$3/4$ cup sugar

INSTRUCTIONS Combine all the ingredients in a blender or food processor. Pour into molds and freeze for at least 6 hours or overnight.

HOW TO STORE IT Freeze up to 3 months. Store in the molds or release, wrap well in waxed paper, and store in a marked sealable plastic bag.

GO FOR THE GRANITA

A light dessert or an elegant palate cleanser, a granita is a cool, refreshing, and highfalutin take on humble frozen pops. To make granita, take any of the nondairy recipes in this chapter, and rather than pouring the cooled mixture into frozen pop molds, pour 3 cups of it into an 8-inch square baking dish. Freeze for 30 minutes. Using a fork, scrape the ice crystals that are forming back and forth. Repeat this process every 30 minutes, 3 or 4 times, until you've made a slushy confection of frozen shards. Once it has achieved the proper consistency, keep stirring it every couple of hours before serving to break up any large ice chunks. Serve in a martini, wine, or champagne glass. Granita does not keep well if you stop paying attention to it, so plan to eat it within a day.

arnold palmer pops

Makes 12 (4-ounce) pops

TIME COMMITMENT
1 day

The beauty of making homemade frozen novelties is that you can create beautiful designs and flavor combinations that simply cannot be store-bought. Sure, you could just make pops out of iced tea—sweet, creamy, and caffeinated—or from a puckery lemonade. But when you layer the two, the whole is more than the sum of its parts. The result is an adult, summertime, frozen explosion of flavor. If you wish to make more than two layers, the sky's the limit. You want each layer to be frozen before adding the next. For four layers in a 4-ounce pop, freeze each layer for at least 90 minutes.

TEA

2 1/4 cups boiling water

2 tea bags

1/4 cup sugar

1/2 cup whole milk

LEMONADE

1/2 cup sugar

2 cups water

1/2 cup freshly squeezed lemon juice (from about 3 or 4 lemons)

INSTRUCTIONS To make the tea, pour the water over the tea bags and steep for 3 to 4 minutes; the tea should be strong. Remove the tea bags and add the sugar, stirring until it's dissolved. Stir in the milk and let cool, for about 30 minutes.

To make the lemonade, combine the sugar and water in a small saucepan, and stir over low heat until the sugar dissolves. Cool, and stir in the lemon juice. Stir well to combine.

To assemble the pops, pour the lemonade into the molds to slightly under the halfway point. Freeze for 2 hours, then add the tea to each mold. Freeze for 6 hours or overnight.

HOW TO STORE IT Freeze up to 3 months. Store in the molds or release, wrap well in waxed paper, and store in a marked sealable plastic bag.

VARIATIONS Other combinations to try include: mango/lemonade, mango/iced tea, watermelon/lemonade, or watermelon/iced tea.

chocolate fudge pops

Makes 7 (4-ounce) pops

TIME COMMITMENT
7 hours

Creamy, chocolaty, and frozen. What could be better? The rich, full-bodied, dark heft of cocoa powder works really well in a frozen state. To me it tastes more like chocolate than melted chocolate itself (go figure). The evaporated milk makes this very much like fudge on a stick. In the winter, rather than cooling the fudge mixture and pouring it into molds, stir it into warm milk and drink it hot—it makes a wonderful, super-dense, rich home-made hot chocolate.

3/4 cup evaporated milk

1/2 cup corn syrup

1 cup water

3 tablespoons golden brown sugar

1/2 cup unsweetened Dutch-process cocoa

1/4 teaspoon kosher salt

1 teaspoon vanilla extract

1 tablespoon unsalted butter

INSTRUCTIONS In a small saucepan, whisk the milk, water, corn syrup, sugar, cocoa, and salt. Heat over medium heat for about 5 minutes, stirring occasionally, until all the solids are dissolved and there are no lumps. Remove from the heat and stir in the vanilla and butter until melted.

Cool the mixture to room temperature. Pour into molds and freeze for about 6 hours, or until solid.

HOW TO STORE IT Freeze up to 3 months. Store in the molds or release, wrap well in waxed paper, and store in a marked sealable plastic bag.

VARIATION Layer the chocolate mixture with the coconut cream pop (page 115) for choco-coconutty goodness.

coconut cream pops

Makes 6 (4-ounce) pops

TIME COMMITMENT
8 hours

I used to be addicted to the frozen coconut cream pops sold at my corner Mexican grocery store. Sure, they're dirt cheap, but I wanted to make my own with great ingredients that don't have to be shipped in a frozen container truck across the border. It took some maneuvering to find the right balance of coconut and dairy milk and to allow the flaked coconut to soak in some chewiness and real coconut flavor. The finished result of this creamsicle is rich and nutty.

1 cup unsweetened coconut milk

3/4 cup evaporated milk

1/2 cup sugar

3/4 cup sweetened flaked coconut

1 teaspoon vanilla extract

INSTRUCTIONS In a small saucepan, combine the coconut milk, evaporated milk, sugar, and coconut. Warm over medium-high heat for about 6 minutes, or until it just starts to bubble. Turn off the heat and cover. Let it sit on top of the stove for 1 hour.

Stir in the vanilla. Pour into molds, and freeze for 6 hours.

HOW TO STORE IT Freeze up to 3 months. Store in the molds or release, wrap well in waxed paper, and store in a marked sealable plastic bag.

VARIATION Layer the coconut mixture with the chocolate fudge pop mixture (page 114) for utter decadence.

burnt salted caramel icies

Makes about 9 (4-ounce)
icies

TIME COMMITMENT
7 hours

This is a challenging recipe because sugar and salt don't take kindly to freezing. Still, the flavor is really pronounced; it's more refreshing than heavy and creamy. Slurp this one up fast, as it melts rather quickly on the stick. In the winter, you can transform this recipe into a remedy for plain old hot chocolate. Rather than freezing the warm mixture, cut it with hot chocolate and drink. The blending of chocolate and caramel is a revolution in cold-weather beverages whose time has come.

1 1/3 cups sugar

3 cups water

1/4 cup heavy whipping cream

1 1/2 teaspoons kosher salt

INSTRUCTIONS Cover the bottom of a heavy skillet with the sugar in an even layer, and place over a medium-high burner. Do not stir until the sugar starts to melt. Cook for about 10 minutes, or until the sugar turns to liquid, gets dark brown, and starts to smoke. Turn the heat down to low.

Slowly and carefully add about 2 tablespoons of the water to the pan. Be careful, as it will splatter a lot. Add the remaining water, a little at a time, until it is thoroughly incorporated into the melted sugar. Turn off the heat. Add the cream and the salt, and mix well.

Cool the mixture completely, then freeze in the molds for 6 hours.

HOW TO STORE IT Freeze up to 3 months. Store in the molds or release, wrap well in waxed paper, and store in a marked sealable plastic bag.

banana cream pops

Makes 6 (4-ounce) pops

TIME COMMITMENT
7 hours

This is more than just a creamy frozen treat; it's also quite tangy thanks to the yogurt. The flavor of ripe banana is prominent, but the Indian spices give it another dimension. If you're not in the mood to wait for it to freeze, these ingredients also make a great smoothie at room temperature. Be sure to use bananas that are quite ripe—ideally those that have about half of their skin covered in black. They have a natural sweetness that really shines through.

4 very ripe bananas

1 cup plain whole milk yogurt

1 teaspoon ground cumin

1 teaspoon ground cinnamon

1 teaspoon vanilla extract

1/4 cup honey

1/2 cup sugar

Pinch of kosher salt

INSTRUCTIONS Combine all the ingredients in a blender or food processor, then pour into molds. Freeze for at least 6 hours or overnight.

HOW TO STORE IT Freeze up to 3 months. Store in the molds or release, wrap well in waxed paper, and store in a marked sealable plastic bag.

11 | unwrap it

MAKING CANDY

While we all grew up with the artificial flavor of store-bought big-brand candy bars, homemade candy is the ultimate crafter's delight. Personally, I'd rather receive a dozen peanut butter cups than a dozen long-stemmed roses any day.

Though the confections explored in this chapter are easy to throw together and devoid of fancy ingredients, they are breathtakingly impressive to share and lend themselves to any kind of decoration the mind can conceive. If you are the kind of cook who likes to make large batches of candies to give over the holidays or for special occasions, these recipes are perfect for you. If you scour thrift stores or craft shops for interesting boxes, tins, and gift bags throughout the year, you'll be December-ready when everyone else is out pounding the mall. No matter what the calendar says, I promise you that these candies will satisfy that primal urge for sweet.

senior mints

Makes about
24 senior mints or about
18 peppermint patties

TIME COMMITMENT
Less than 4 hours

There are two kinds of chocolate-covered mints in this world: those that are addictive, sweet, and the stuff of movie theater memories, and those that are cloying and heavy with cream. This candy is the former variety, but all grown up: super minty, light, and devoid of the chemical additives typically found in their familiar shelf-stable younger cousin. This recipe merits better-than-average chocolate, such as Valrhona, Dagoba, or Scharffen Berger, which might require a trip to a gourmet market. To gift these, present them in a cellophane bag tied with a decorative ribbon or in a small tin box. For bonus points pair them with Peanut Butter Cups (page 125), Coconut Almond Candy Bars (page 123), and cocoa-dusted Marshmallows (page 101).

2 cups confectioners' sugar

1/4 teaspoon kosher salt

1 tablespoon light corn syrup

1 tablespoon vegetable oil

1 tablespoon peppermint oil or extract

1 tablespoon water

1 1/2 cups good-quality dark chocolate chips or chunks

INSTRUCTIONS Combine the sugar, salt, corn syrup, vegetable oil, and peppermint oil in a large bowl. Beat with an electric mixer at medium speed, adding the water a little at a time as necessary, until the mixture becomes a malleable dough.

Pinch off 1-inch long pieces of the dough and roll into balls. Place the balls on a rimmed baking sheet and freeze for 20 minutes.

About 3 minutes before removing the mints from the freezer, place the chocolate chips in a microwave-safe bowl and heat, on high power, for 1 minute. Stir with a fork, and microwave for 1 minute more. Stir again, and micro-

wave for another 30 to 60 seconds, until the chocolate is completely melted and very shiny and you can dribble it from the fork in long ribbons.

Remove a few mints from the freezer at a time. Working as quickly as possible with a spoon (or 2 forks), roll 1 mint at a time through the chocolate, covering the ball completely with a thin layer of chocolate, and transfer to a rack placed over a second rimmed baking sheet. After 4 to 5 minutes, when the chocolate starts to stiffen, heat the chocolate in the microwave for 1 minute, then stir well before resuming coating. Continue working until all of the mints are coated in chocolate.

Leave the chocolate-coated mints at room temperature for about 2 hours, or until firm.

HOW TO STORE IT These mints will keep up to 2 weeks when stored in an airtight container. Try freezing a few to enjoy on a hot day—though once you've had them in the freezer, you won't want to return them to room temperature again.

VARIATION It's a snap to form these little bonbons into peppermint patties. Pinch 1 1/2- to 2-inch-long pieces of dough, roll into balls, and flatten between your palms to a thickness of 1/4 to 1/2 inch. Place the disks on the baking sheet and follow the instructions above. Voilà! Peppermint patties.

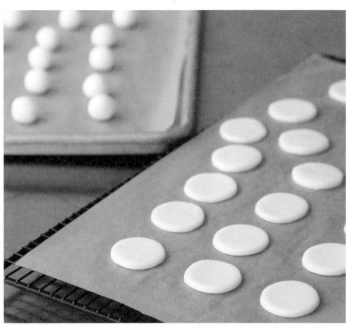

toffee

Makes about 1 1/2 pounds

TIME COMMITMENT
3 hours

Nothing in this world is bad when a pound of butter and a hammer are involved. Besides indulging in butter, I like using a bit of brown sugar in this recipe to give this toffee a more complex butterscotch kick. This is toffee at its best—rich, flavorful, crunchy, and chewy. This recipe calls for the use of a candy thermometer, since it is essential for the toffee to reach a specific temperature before it's ready to mold. If you prefer to bite into a thin wafer rather than a hefty chunk, thinly spread the toffee over a parchment paper–covered baking sheet, rather than a baking dish. If you plan to gift this, be mindful of toffee's sticky nature. Presenting the toffee in cupcake liners will keep the pieces from clumping together.

2/3 cup roasted and salted almonds, peanuts, or walnuts, or a combination, chopped

1/3 cup chocolate chips or chopped chocolate (optional)

1 pound unsalted butter

1 1/2 cups granulated sugar

1/2 cup golden brown sugar

1/2 teaspoon kosher salt

1/2 teaspoon vanilla extract

INSTRUCTIONS To prepare an 8 by 8-inch baking dish, oil all the way up the sides, line with enough parchment paper to hang over the edge and act as a handle later, add another layer of oil over the paper, and scatter the nuts and chocolate (if desired) evenly across the bottom.

In a saucepan on medium-low heat, melt the butter, then add the granulated sugar, brown sugar, and salt. Stir with a wooden spoon to combine and to help the sugar melt. Cook for about 15 to 20 minutes, or until the mixture reaches 290°F.

Once the mixture reaches the right temperature, turn off the heat and allow to cool for a couple of minutes, until the bubbling stops. The mixture will be as viscous as pudding and a deep, tawny color. At this point, stir in the vanilla. Pour the mixture evenly over the nuts and chocolate in the prepared pan.

Let cool for about 10 to 15 minutes, then score in 6 rows both horizontally and vertically. The toffee will not break on these lines, but they will help when you shatter it later.

Leave the toffee at room temperature for about 2 hours, until hardened. Pour off any excess oil that has floated to the top and discard. Lift the toffee from the pan and invert onto a clean kitchen towel. Wrap the toffee in the towel, and go at it with the hammer, breaking the toffee into rough pieces.

HOW TO STORE IT Store toffee in a single layer or in layers separated by waxed paper. It will keep for at least 10 days when stored airtight at room temperature.

coconut almond candy bars

Makes 12 to 14 bars

TIME COMMITMENT
5 hours

Sometimes you feel like a nut. Sometimes you don't. But rare is the moment when you don't feel like devouring a chewy coconut bar, offset with the well-rounded salt of toasted almonds slathered in excellent chocolate. If you are presenting these candy bars as gifts, they offer an opportunity to get creative with packaging. First wrap each candy bar individually in plastic wrap, then wrap them with a decorative wrapper of your own design. Or throw a few into a cellophane bag and affix a custom label to it.

2 large egg whites

1/2 cup sugar

1 teaspoon vanilla extract

1/2 teaspoon kosher salt

2 cups sweetened flaked coconut

24 to 28 whole roasted salted almonds

2 cups chocolate chips or chopped chocolate

INSTRUCTIONS To make the bars, preheat the oven to 350°F, and prepare a rimmed baking sheet with a thin sheen of oil.

Combine the egg whites, sugar, vanilla, and salt in a bowl and mix with a fork. You don't have to beat the whites—just make sure the sugar, vanilla, and salt are well incorporated. Fold in the coconut. The batter will be stiff, like oatmeal.

Spoon about 2 tablespoons of the batter into your hand, and shape into a 1 1/2-inch-long log. Press 2 almonds into the top of the log, and place on the prepared baking sheet. Follow suit with the remainder of the batter. You should have at least 12 bars.

Bake for 13 to 17 minutes, or until the bars are just brown at the edges. Let cool 1 minute, transfer to a wire rack, and leave for about 30 minutes, or until completely cool.

To coat the bars, prepare the baking sheet with a sheet of waxed paper or parchment paper, and have it at the ready.

In a microwave-safe bowl, heat the chocolate on high for 1 minute, and stir well to distribute the heat. Heat for 1 minute more, and stir again. Heat for an additional 30 to 60 seconds, stirring thoroughly with a fork. The chocolate should be melted and quite satiny, and you should be able to drop it in ribbons from the end of the fork.

Using 2 forks, drop a bar into the chocolate and coat lightly on all sides, then quickly transfer to the waxed paper. Dip the remaining bars. If the chocolate layer gets too thick or your chocolate starts to get stiff, heat the chocolate for 1 minute more, stirring well to distribute the heat.

Leave the finished candies at room temperature for about 4 hours, or until completely cool.

HOW TO STORE IT Store in an airtight tin or in a sealable plastic bag, at room temperature, up to 2 weeks.

peanut butter cups

Makes 12 individual cups

TIME COMMITMENT
5 hours

Chocolate and peanut butter together create one of my favorite candy confections. This version has everything going for it: a sweet and salty peanut butter filling and the opportunity for a high-quality chocolate of your own choosing to balance it out. No actual cooking is required here, making this a good choice for making chocolate when the weather is scorching. For better flavor, roast your own peanuts or freshen roasted peanuts in a heavy skillet until lightly browned. You'll need paper (or silicone) cupcake pan inserts for this recipe, which, along with the finished product, create a handsome gift.

FILLING

1 1/3 cups fresh roasted and salted peanuts

2 teaspoons honey

1 teaspoon neutral vegetable oil, like canola or sunflower

2 tablespoons confectioners' sugar

1/2 teaspoon vanilla extract

1/2 teaspoon kosher salt

COATING

2 cups chocolate chips or chopped chocolate

INSTRUCTIONS To make the peanut butter filling, place the liners in your cupcake pan, and have a holding dish standing by. In a food processor, puree the peanuts for 3 to 4 minutes, until very smooth. Add the honey, oil, sugar, vanilla, and salt and puree until completely combined, scraping down the sides as you work.

Take about 2 teaspoons of the peanut butter mixture into your clean hands, roll into a ball, and flatten into a disk that will fit into the center of the cupcake liner but not touch the sides. Shape the remaining 11 centers. The peanut butter should be evenly distributed.

To prepare the coating, in a microwave-safe bowl heat the chocolate on high for 1 minute, and stir well with a fork to distribute the heat. Heat for 1 minute more, and stir again. Heat for an additional 30 to 60 seconds, stirring thoroughly. The chocolate should be melted and quite satiny, and you should be able to drop it in ribbons from the end of the fork.

To assemble the cups, working quickly, spoon about 2 teaspoons of melted chocolate into the bottom of each liner, being careful to coat the bottom in a complete, thin layer, and to coat the sides about halfway up. Gently drop each of the peanut butter disks into the center of a cup, and give it a gentle tap to secure it in the chocolate (but don't push it all the way through to the bottom). Cover each center with an additional teaspoon of chocolate, covering the top completely and allowing it to surround the sides of the peanut butter, enclosing it completely. Gently smooth out the tops with the back of the spoon or by giving the pan a gentle shake. Let sit, undisturbed, for at least 4 hours, until the cups harden completely.

HOW TO STORE IT Devour immediately, or store up to 2 weeks in an airtight container. Do not refrigerate.

12 | drink it

HARD AND SOFT BEVERAGES

Making your own interesting libations, alcoholic and otherwise, has a lot of benefits. They look and sound fancy, when in truth all you did was blend a few ingredients or throw some high-quality flavorings into a jar. The recipes in this chapter are absolutely foolproof: it's nearly impossible to burn, under-cook, or ruin a homemade beverage, even for the novice cook. A homemade beverage makes drinking at home—or in someone else's home—feel special.

When it comes to infusing your own spirits, know that it should be a cheap buzz. Buy the most economical vodka or brandy you can find. This is one of those rare occasions in which the very best ingredients aren't always a necessity for the very best results. Spend your money instead on top-quality flavoring agents—fresh fruit, whole spices, and high-quality vanilla beans—because that's where your efforts will pay off.

jamaican ginger beer

Makes about 8 cups

TIME COMMITMENT
Less than 1 hour

Whenever I headed to South Florida to see my mother, I paid a visit to Daddy's, a hole-in-the-wall Jamaican restaurant that served excellent jerk chicken. But his ginger beer—oh, his ginger beer—was the reason I kept going to this dank joint. I asked Daddy for the recipe, but only after multiple visits did he share his amazing secret for one of the most refreshing beverages in drink history. Sadly, Daddy and his restaurant just disappeared one day. However, in my kitchen and now in yours, his legendary ginger beer lives on. This ginger beer is authentic—and very strong. Serve it in a tall glass over ice, or cut with soda water, limeade, or ginger ale, or spike with a shot (or two) of cold vodka or dark rum.

$2^{1}/_{2}$ pounds fresh ginger, roughly peeled

4 cups water, divided

1 cup freshly squeezed lime juice (from 8 to 10 limes)

$2^{1}/_{2}$ to 3 cups sugar

INSTRUCTIONS In a blender or food processor, liquefy the ginger and 2 cups of the water for 3 minutes, then strain the juice into a large bowl or pitcher. Transfer the ginger pulp back to the blender or processor, add another cup of the water, and liquefy again. Strain again, adding the liquid to the first batch. Again transfer the pulp along with another cup of water, liquefy again, and add to the liquid. Press on the solids as much as possible to squeeze out as much of the juice as you can.

Once the ginger has given up all that it's got, discard the mashed solids. Add the lime juice and $2^{1}/_{2}$ cups of the sugar. Mix well and taste. Add more sugar, a few tablespoons or so at a time, until it reaches your preferred sweetness. Drink immediately or chill.

HOW TO STORE IT Refrigerate up to 3 weeks. Shake before serving.

chai

Makes 3¹/2 cups

TIME COMMITMENT
1 hour

Soy chai, cream chai, chai latte . . . the American urban coffee shop has fully acquired and bastardized the Indian classic, spiced it up, bottled it, and made it sickeningly sweet and ready-to-pour. Rather than going out for that daily spiced cuppa, make your own. When preparing chai, use whole spices, because the flavor is fresher and they will be easier to fish out of the brew later. Tie them up in an empty tea bag or plan to strain them out at the end. Serve chai warm, chilled over ice, or even frozen as an ice pop or slushed into a granita (page 112).

3 cups water

4 large slices fresh ginger

¹/2 vanilla bean, split lengthwise

1 (2-inch) piece cinnamon stick

¹/2 star anise

4 cloves

8 cardamom pods, cracked

¹/2 teaspoon black peppercorns

2 tea bags, black or Darjeeling

1 cup milk, cream, or soy milk

1 tablespoon granulated sugar

2 tablespoons golden brown sugar

Fresh grated nutmeg or dried nutmeg powder, for garnish

INSTRUCTIONS Pour the water into a saucepan and add the ginger, vanilla bean, and cinnamon stick. Bring to a boil, reduce the heat, and simmer, covered, for 15 minutes.

Add the star anise, cloves, cardamom, and peppercorns, and continue to simmer for an additional 15 minutes.

Turn off the heat, toss in the tea bags, cover, and steep for 3 to 5 minutes. Remove all the solids, and squeeze out their liquid. Stir in the milk, granulated sugar, and brown sugar. Stir to combine and return to medium-low heat, just until heated through thoroughly; don't let it boil. Garnish with nutmeg and serve immediately.

HOW TO STORE IT Refrigerate up to 1 week and reheat as needed.

orange-flavored vodka

Makes 3½ cups

TIME COMMITMENT
5 weeks

Vodka is a frequently used spirit for infusion because it is neutral—that is, it has very little flavor of its own and plays nicely with whatever flavors drop in, namely citrus fruit, stone fruit, and dried fruit; fresh herbs and nuts; and fresh spices. For those just starting to experiment with infusions, orange is a great fruit to begin with: it is readily available, and it has a pleasing flavor that works well in numerous cocktails and pairs beautifully with food (try sipping it with a piece of dark chocolate). This drink can be enjoyed at room temperature or cold.

PREP AHEAD You'll need a clean, odor-free, wide-mouthed glass jar with a tight-fitting lid for the infusion process. However, if you are planning on giving this as a gift or serving it at your next party, consider pouring the finished infusion into an attractive bottle with a tight-fitting cap. Prepare labels for the jar and bottle listing contents and date prepared.

    1 quart inexpensive vodka
    4 sweet oranges, like navels

INSTRUCTIONS Pour the vodka into your prepared jar. Scrub the oranges well under running water, and dry. Slice each orange into 4 to 6 pieces, and submerge in the vodka. Label the jar, cap tightly, and store in a cool, dark place, shaking it once a day, for 2 weeks.

Strain the liquid through a fine mesh sieve or paper coffee filter to remove all of the fruit and its particles. Return the strained vodka to its jar, cover tightly again, and return to its cool, dark place for 3 more weeks to age and mature the flavor.

HOW TO STORE IT Keep it away from heat and light. Refrigerate or freeze almost indefinitely.

VARIATIONS For the oranges, substitute 2 cups fresh strawberries, 8 large stems crushed basil, or 12 dried hot chiles.

orange liqueur

Makes about 5 cups

TIME COMMITMENT
8 weeks

Once you've mastered the basic infusion, then it's time to make a basic cordial (also called a liqueur), which is, essentially, a flavored spirit with added sugar introduced via a simple syrup. The key to this recipe is to infuse the booze, remove the solids, and add the syrup to the infused alcohol before the second aging period. You can make the simple syrup up to a month in advance and keep it refrigerated; if you prepare it right before using it in this recipe, make sure it is completely cool before adding it to the alcohol. Enjoy this cordial at room temperature or cold.

PREP AHEAD You'll need a clean, odor-free, wide-mouthed glass jar with a tight-fitting lid for the infusion process. However, if you are planning on giving this liqueur as a gift or serving it at your next party, consider pouring the infusion into an attractive bottle with a tight-fitting cap. Prepare labels for the jar and bottle listing contents and date prepared.

1 cup sugar
1 cup water
4 cups Orange-Flavored Vodka (page 131), solids discarded

INSTRUCTIONS To make a simple syrup, combine the sugar and water in a small saucepan, and heat just until all of the sugar is dissolved. Cool completely.

Pour the orange vodka into the jar. To sweeten, start by adding 3/4 cup of the syrup; stir completely, and adjust the sweetness to your taste. Note, however, that the infusion will get sweeter as it ages. Label the jar, cover tightly again, and let mellow for 6 weeks in a cool dark place before drinking, as the flavor will continue to evolve.

HOW TO STORE IT Cap tightly and refrigerate, or store in a cool, dark place almost indefinitely.

toasted walnut brandy

Makes 4 cups

TIME COMMITMENT
5 weeks

While vodka is merely a mirror for the flavors that it carries, an infused brandy reflects the sepia tones of honey and amber and a slightly woody flavor. For infusing brandy, think fall flavors—slightly more earthen tastes like apple, nut, and dried fruit. This libation may be enjoyed at room temperature or cold.

PREP AHEAD You'll need a clean, odor-free, wide-mouthed glass jar with a tight-fitting lid for the infusion process. However, if you are planning on giving this liqueur as a gift or serving it at your next party, consider pouring the infusion into an attractive bottle with a tight-fitting cap. Prepare labels for the jar and bottle listing contents and date prepared.

4 cups inexpensive brandy
1 cup unsalted walnuts

INSTRUCTIONS Toast the walnuts in a heavy skillet over high heat for 4 to 5 minutes, or until they are fully browned. Transfer them immediately to a cold plate. Once they are cooled completely, chop the walnuts. Pour the brandy into your prepared jar. Add the walnuts. Label the jar, cap tightly, and store in a cool, dark place, shaking it once a day, for 2 weeks.

Strain the brandy through a fine mesh sieve or paper coffee filter to remove all of the walnuts and their particles. Return the strained brandy to its jar, cover tightly again, and return to its cool, dark place for 3 more weeks.

HOW TO STORE IT Keep it away from heat and light. Refrigerate or freeze almost indefinitely.

VARIATIONS For the toasted walnuts, substitute 1 cup raisins or 1 cup toasted, unsalted almonds.

winter solstice brew

Makes 4 cups

TIME COMMITMENT
5 weeks

Blending your own boozy flavor combinations is a fun, low-risk way to be kitchen creative, and a great way to show off your DIY chops. These winter flavors are sure to give eggnog a run for its money as your favorite way to keep warm in December. The vanilla adds a light natural sweetness, and the fruit and spice truly make this infusion smooth and easy on the palate. Enjoy this brew at room temperature or cold, or add a shot of it to hot apple cider and drink warm.

PREP AHEAD You'll need a clean, odor-free, wide-mouthed glass jar with a tight-fitting lid for the infusion process. However, if you are planning on giving this liqueur as a gift or serving it at your next party, consider pouring the infusion into an attractive bottle with a tight-fitting cap. Prepare labels for the jar and bottle listing contents and date prepared.

4 cups brandy

2 star anise

1 (8-inch) piece cinnamon stick

1 (8-inch) piece vanilla bean, sliced lengthwise

4 small sweet navel oranges, scrubbed, dried, and chopped into 4 to 6 pieces

24 black peppercorns

INSTRUCTIONS Combine all the ingredients in the jar. Label the jar, cap tightly, and store in a cool, dark place for 2 weeks, shaking daily.

Strain the brew through a fine mesh sieve or paper coffee filter to remove the fruit and spices. Return the infusion to its jar, cover tightly again, and return to its cool, dark place for 3 weeks.

HOW TO STORE IT Refrigerate, or store in a cool, dark pantry, almost indefinitely.

hot and sweet liqueur

Makes about 5 cups

TIME COMMITMENT
8 weeks

This is an unusual and heady mix; admittedly, it's not for everyone. The ginger and the dried chiles give this a rugged, exuberant kick, but the sugar and carrot give it some nice color and a softer edge. You can make the simple syrup up to a month in advance and keep it refrigerated. If you prepare it right before using it in this recipe, make sure it is completely cool before adding it to the alcohol. Try this as an aperitif to stimulate the appetite at room temperature or cold.

PREP AHEAD You'll need a clean, odor-free, wide-mouthed glass jar with a tight-fitting lid for the infusion process. However, if you are planning on giving this liqueur as a gift or serving it at your next party, consider pouring the infusion into an attractive bottle with a tight-fitting cap. Prepare labels for the jar and bottle listing contents and date prepared.

    1 cup sugar
    1 cup water
    4 cups vodka
    4 large carrots, cut into 2-inch chunks
    4 (1-inch) pieces fresh ginger
    6 dried red chiles

INSTRUCTIONS To make a simple syrup, combine the sugar and water in a small saucepan, and heat just until all of the sugar is dissolved. Cool completely.

Pour the vodka into the jar. Add the carrot, ginger, and chiles, and infuse for 2 weeks in a cool, dark place, shaking daily. Discard the solids, and return the infused vodka to its jar.

To sweeten the liqueur, start by adding $3/4$ cup of the syrup; stir completely, and adjust the sweetness to your taste. (Note, however, that the liqueur will get sweeter with age.) Label the jar, cover tightly again, and allow it to mellow in a cool dark place for 6 weeks before drinking, as the flavor will continue to evolve.

HOW TO STORE IT Cap tightly and refrigerate, or store in a cool, dark place almost indefinitely.

fruit and nut brandy

Makes 4 cups

TIME COMMITMENT
5 weeks

A pal of mine turned me on to a cocktail called Nuts and Berries—equal parts hazelnut Frangelica and raspberry Chambord. I loved the combination (think peanut butter and jelly) but thought that it was a little too cloying to drink for more than just a sip or two. That libation was what I had in mind while crafting Fruit and Nut Brandy, which has a lighter body. The sweetness of the fruit is subtle and the well-rounded flavors from the nuts give this infusion nice texture and a hearty chew without too much sugar. Try it with a plate of fruits, nuts, and earthy, nutty cheeses, or enjoy it anytime at room temperature or served cold.

PREP AHEAD You'll need a clean, odor-free, wide-mouthed glass jar with a tight-fitting lid for the infusion process. However, if you are planning on giving this liqueur as a gift or serving it at your next party, consider pouring the infusion into an attractive bottle with a tight-fitting cap. Prepare labels for the jar and bottle listing contents and date prepared.

  4 cups brandy
  32 dried cranberries
  12 dates, sliced lengthwise, with their pits
  4 raw unsalted almonds, chopped
  20 raw unsalted walnuts, chopped

INSTRUCTIONS Combine all the ingredients in the jar. Label the jar, cap tightly, and store in a cool, dark place for 2 weeks, shaking daily.

  Strain the liquid through a fine mesh sieve or paper coffee filter to remove the fruit and nuts. Return the strained brandy to its jar, cover tightly again, and return to its cool, dark place for 3 weeks.

HOW TO STORE IT Refrigerate, or store in a cool, dark pantry, almost indefinitely.

Opposite: (L–R) Winter Solstice Brew (page 134), Rumkirschen (page 141), Fruit and Nut Brandy, Hot and Sweet Liqueur (page 135), Limoncello (page 139)

potent iced tea with lemon cordial

Makes about 5 cups

TIME COMMITMENT
8 weeks

Tea lovers will find this an interesting exercise, because the flavor of tea is rarely made alcoholic (save for that Long Island variety, which has no actual tea in it). When working with tea infusions, it's important not to let tea leaves soak more than 12 hours, because they can imbue a bitterness to the end result. You can make the simple syrup up to a month ahead of time. If you prepare it right before using it in this recipe, make sure it is completely cool before adding it to the alcohol. Serve this one very cold and over ice, or spike it into a glass of real iced tea for a summer buzz and bliss.

PREP AHEAD You'll need a clean, odor-free, wide-mouthed glass jar with a tight-fitting lid for the infusion process. However, if you are planning on giving this liqueur as a gift or serving it at your next party, consider pouring the infusion into an attractive bottle with a tight-fitting cap. Prepare labels for the jar and bottle listing contents and date prepared.

1 cup sugar

1 cup water

4 cups brandy

2 teaspoons tea leaves

1 large lemon

INSTRUCTIONS To make a simple syrup, combine the sugar and water in a small saucepan, and heat just until all of the sugar is dissolved. Cool completely.

Pour the brandy into the jar, and add the tea leaves. Infuse at room temperature for 6 to 8 hours. Strain through a sieve and discard the tea leaves, and return the infused brandy to its jar. Slice the lemon, add it to the infusion, and store for 2 weeks. Strain through a sieve, discard the lemon, and return the brandy to its jar.

To sweeten the cordial, start by adding 3/4 cup of the syrup; stir completely, and adjust the sweetness to your taste. (Note that the cordial will get sweeter with age.) Label the jar, cover tightly again, and let mellow for 6 weeks before drinking.

HOW TO STORE IT It will last almost indefinitely refrigerated or stored in a cool, dark place.

limoncello

Makes about 3 cups

TIME COMMITMENT
8 weeks

In college, we combined lemonade powder mix with cheap vodka and called it a Sledge-hammer. In the 1990s, it was served at bars for $12 and known as a Lemon Drop. The merger of lemon and vodka is addictive because of its fresh flavor and zing. Take ten steps back into the history of the cocktail and you'll find limoncello, a traditional home-made Italian liqueur often drunk ice-cold and in shots at the end of a meal. Most recipes use just the lemon zest, but the juice adds a freshness that is outstanding. Avoid using Meyer lemons for this liqueur—they're not tart enough. Serve limoncello ice-cold.

PREP AHEAD You'll need a clean, odor-free, wide-mouthed glass jar with a tight-fitting lid for the infusion process. However, if you are planning on giving this liqueur as a gift or serving it at your next party, consider pouring the infusion into an attractive bottle with a tight-fitting cap. Prepare labels for the jar and bottle listing contents and date prepared.

- 8 lemons
- 1 1/2 cups vodka
- 1 cup sugar
- 1 cup water

INSTRUCTIONS Peel the zest from 4 of the lemons with a zester or vegetable peeler, trying to avoid as much of the white pith as you can. Pour the vodka into the jar, and add the zest. Seal and label the jar, and let sit for 2 weeks, shaking daily, then strain out and discard the lemon zest.

To make a simple syrup, combine the sugar and water in a small saucepan, and heat just until all of the sugar is dissolved. It's imperative to let this cool completely. You can expedite the cooling process by moving the syrup to a glass bowl and stirring constantly, or refrigerating it for at least 30 minutes.

Squeeze the remaining 4 lemons, remove the seeds, and add their juice to the syrup.

Add the lemon syrup to the infused vodka and allow it to mellow for 6 weeks.

HOW TO STORE IT Store in a cool, dark place or in the freezer almost indefinitely. The high alcohol content will keep it from freezing.

limoncello di crema

Makes about 3 1/2 cups

TIME COMMITMENT
8 weeks

Whereas limoncello is pure acid and fruit, here, the addition of milk makes the finished product unctuous like melted ice cream. This beverage is dessert for me: it's sweet, creamy, and lemony and needs nothing more than biscotti to be complete. Also, try drizzling it over vanilla ice cream. Avoid using Meyer lemons because they're not tart enough. Serve this in ice-cold shots at the end of a satisfying meal, but be careful since it goes down quite smoothly but really packs a punch.

PREP AHEAD You'll need a clean, odor-free, wide-mouthed glass jar with a tight-fitting lid for the infusion process. However, if you are planning on giving this liqueur as a gift or serving it at your next party, consider pouring the infusion into an attractive bottle with a tight-fitting cap. Prepare labels for the jar and bottle listing contents and date prepared.

> 4 lemons
> 1 1/2 cups vodka
> 1 cup sugar
> 1 cup water
> 2 cups whole milk

INSTRUCTIONS Peel the zest from the lemons with a zester or vegetable peeler, trying to avoid as much of the white pith as you can. Pour the vodka into the jar, and add the zest. Seal and label the jar, and let sit for 2 weeks, shaking daily, then strain out and discard the lemon zest.

To make a simple syrup, combine the sugar and water in a small saucepan, and heat just until all of the sugar is dissolved.

Add the milk to the syrup. Simmer, uncovered, for about 15 minutes, or until the liquid reduces by half. It's imperative to let this cool completely. You can expedite the cooling process by stirring constantly, or refrigerating it for at least 30 minutes.

Add the milky syrup to the infused vodka, shake well, and allow it to sit for 6 weeks. Transfer to the freezer and serve fully chilled.

HOW TO STORE IT Store in a cool, dark place or in the freezer almost indefinitely. The high alcohol content will keep it from freezing.

rumkirschen

Makes 3¹/₂ cups

TIME COMMITMENT
3 days or more

This eastern European liqueur is made from tart Morello cherries and rum. Morello cherries, a varietal of sour cherry, are dark red and have an unusual and pleasant sour flavor. They can be difficult to find, but try specialty stores such as Trader Joe's and eastern European markets, or order them through online retailers. I wrote this recipe using a 20-ounce jar of cherries from Trader Joe's. Any size jar will work as long as you keep in mind that you want a syrup-to-rum ratio of 2 to 1, and adjust the amount of rum accordingly. Although the infused cherries are fantastic eaten alone, consider sautéing them with fresh pineapple in a little butter and brown sugar. It makes an outstanding dessert, especially when paired with ice cream and/or pound cake. Some imbibe the cherry liqueur in a cup of hot tea, but I much prefer it cold and straight up, or cut with 7-Up or soda water.

PREP AHEAD You'll need 2 clean, odor-free, wide-mouthed glass jars with tight-fitting lids for the infusion process (you can reuse the jar the cherries came in, if you like). However, if you are planning on giving this liqueur as a gift or serving it at your next party, consider pouring the infusion into an attractive bottle with a tight-fitting cap. Prepare labels for the jar and bottle listing contents and date prepared.

1 (20-ounce) jar Morello cherries
About 1 cup amber or dark rum (anything but white)

INSTRUCTIONS Drain the cherries into a bowl, reserving the syrup. Pour the syrup into a Pyrex measuring cup; you should have about 2 cups. Pour half the syrup into each of the two jars and divide the drained cherries evenly between the jars. Pour ¹/₂ cup of rum into each jar.

Cover the jars tightly, label, and shake gently to combine. Refrigerate for at least 3 days, though the flavors develop more fully the longer you let the jars sit.

HOW TO STORE IT Keep refrigerated. The syrup and fruit will last almost indefinitely.

index

C